D0353314

PHOTOSHOP
Filter Effects Cookbook
for Digital Photographers

PHOTOSHOP Filter Effects Cookbook
for Digital Photographers

Roger Pring

ILEX

Contents

PHOTOSHOP FILTER EFFECTS COOKBOOK

Copyright © 2006 The Ilex Press Limited

First published in the United Kingdom in 2006 by:

I L E X

3 St Andrews Place

Lewes, East Sussex

BN7 1UP

Publisher: Alastair Campbell

Executive Publisher: Sophie Collins

Creative Director: Peter Bridgewater

Managing Editor: Tom Mugridge

Project Editor: Ben Renow-Clarke

Art Director: Julie Weir

Designer: Jonathan Raimes

Junior Designer: Stephen Minns

I L E X is an imprint of the Ilex Press Ltd

Visit us on the Web at:

www.ilex-press.com

This book was conceived by:

I L E X , Cambridge, England

Any copy of this book issued by the publisher as a paperback is sold subject to the condition that it shall not by way of trade or otherwise be lent, resold, hired out, or otherwise circulated without the publisher's prior consent in any form of binding or cover other than that in which it is published and without a similar condition including these words being imposed on a subsequent purchaser.

British Library Cataloguing-in-publication data.

A catalogue record for this book is available from the British Library.

ISBN 1-904705-67-7

All rights reserved. No part of this publication may be reproduced or used in any form, or by any means – graphic, electronic, or mechanical, including photocopying, recording, or information storage-and-retrieval systems – without the prior permission of the publisher.

Printed and bound in China

For more information on this title please visit:

www.web-linked.com/fifxuk

Introduction

You may get into the Photoshop Filters menu out of curiosity, or be propelled there on a rescue mission. In either case, you have a daunting collection of 109 filters from which to choose. The great majority of these filters offer enhancements that take the form of painterly or graphic simulations, texture effects, and distortions. The rest are designed to deal with perceived flaws in the photographic original. This book examines all of these filters on their merits and also suggests alternative ways to use them separately and in combination. Some filters work perfectly right out of the box, while others need help, either from additional filters or by means of a different Photoshop technique.

For each of the 13 groups of regular filters, a different original is treated at various settings by each filter. Where the conventional image doesn't fully reveal the action of an individual filter, an additional multicolored target image has been used to demonstrate its effect. To show further possibilities, each filter is then used in a different context. In some cases, there are more effective ways of achieving the filter's objectives without using the filter at all. In others, extreme filter settings can produce unexpected and useful effects. With such a large number of available filters and uncountable combinations of adjustments, it's clear that every possibility cannot be covered in a book of this size.

There is a group of four filters (small applications, in effect) at the top of the filter menu—Extract, Liquify, Pattern Generator, and Vanishing Point. For the purposes of this book, they have been added to the "Other" filter group, which is covered at the end of the book.

FILTER GALLERY

Fewer than half of the filters in Photoshop appear in its Filter Gallery. These filters will automatically open in the Filter Gallery window, or you can choose Filter gallery at the top of the Filter menu. Click on a folder in the center window and select a filter—the panel shows the familiar controls, but there are some extra features. To see the effect of two filters simultaneously, click on the turned-page icon at bottom right. Initially, this duplicates the previous filter, so click on another filter to change it. In the image below, the first selection was Cutout, and we followed this with Film Grain.

Click on the eyeball icon to show or hide the effect of each filter. You can continue adding filter layers until the desired effect is reached—the upper limit is generous at over 100. In practical terms, four different filters are probably enough. The trash can is nearby, at the bottom right, to delete unwanted filters from the cumulative stack. In future versions of Photoshop, we can hope for intensity controls for individual filters in the stack when used as a group of two or more. For now, they are either on or off. Curiously, the filters in the gallery differ slightly in use from the filters that are not in the gallery. With the latter, you can reset the filter to its previous state by hitting the Cancel button while holding down the Alt/Option key. That's still true with the gallery filters, but, if you cancel while holding down the Ctrl/Cmd key, all of the gallery filters are returned to their factory settings.

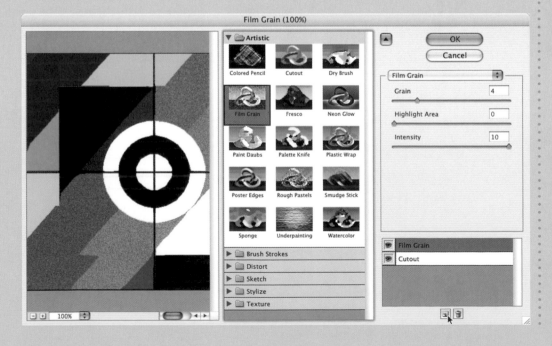

PHOTO FILTERS

In the Image menu, you'll find Photo Filter in the Adjustments section. The first six filters are precise reproductions of some of the original Kodak, Wratten, and Fuji correction filters; the rest comprise a varied selection of colors. The last filter in the group, Underwater, is not intended to reduce the excess blue-green light that plagues underwater photography, but to simulate it on any Image. You can use these filters in the conventional way, directly on the image, but it's usually better to use a Photo Filter adjustment layer (see below). That way, you can try all 20 filters without modifying the pixels in the original image.

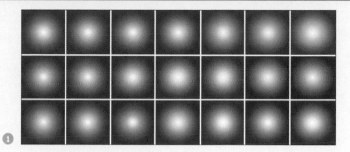

① The filters are set by default to operate at 25% strength. Here they have been used on a 50% gray-to-white gradient at that default setting. In the top row, from left to right:

No filter applied; Warming Filter (85); Warming Filter (LBA); Warming Filter (81); Cooling Filter (80); Cooling Filter (LBB); Cooling Filter (82). Second row: Red; Orange; Yellow; Green; Cyan; Blue; Violet. Third row: Magenta; Sepia; Deep Red; Deep Blue; Deep Emerald; Deep Yellow; Underwater.

The original 85A and 85B filters were designed to enable the use of tungsten light (indoor/photoflood) film in daylight conditions. The film was (and still is) made with an inherent blue cast to counteract the strongly yellow color of the indoor lamps. Unfiltered use of indoor film outdoors would result in an overall blue cast. The 85A filter reduced the apparent color temperature from 5500°K (cool and blue) to 3400°K (warmer and more red), the 85B made it even warmer and redder. Today, these filters are rarely part of the digital photographer's arsenal as most digital cameras compensate automatically for variations in color temperature. Use these filters to adjust your images when the camera's compensation is not quite right, or to correct scans from transparencies shot on the wrong type of film. You can use these filters instead to warm up digital images that appear excessively cool, or to correct scans from transparencies shot on the incorrect film.

② Here, the landscape shows elevated levels of blue due to the atmospheric scattering of UV light.

③ To create an adjustment layer, click on the black-and-white disk icon at the foot of the Layers window and choose Photo Filter from the fly-out menu. Alternatively, go to the main menu and select **Image** > **Adjustments** > **Photo Filter**. In either case, the resulting dialog box offers the currently available adjustment layers, including Photo Filter.

④ Choose the relevant filter and adjust its density if necessary. The default 25% is usually sufficient—higher values generally produce an objectionable cast.

⑤ If you want to try combinations of filters, it's useful to name the adjustment layers.

⑥ The Warming filter (85) successfully removes much of the blue cast without upsetting the overall color balance.

7

The Artistic filters

For the photographer, the 15 effects in the Artistic filters suite offer simulations of a wide range of painterly techniques. You'll quickly discover which ones are the most useful—and the range of subjects that will benefit from their application. You'll learn equally quickly that some of the filters resemble their real-life counterparts in name only. Leading the virtuous pack are Colored Pencil, Paint Daubs, Cutout, Poster Edges, and Watercolor, with Neon Glow, Palette Knife, and Sponge battling for last place. There are other "artistic" or "painterly" filters hidden away under different sections of this book, and we've added cross-references where appropriate to help you find them.

All of these filters are equipped with at least three sliders, so we've narrowed down the available combinations to concentrate on practical settings.

The Artistic filters

page 8—Palette Knife

page 10—Colored Pencil

page 12—Cutout

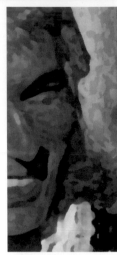
page 15—Sponge

page 16—Dry Brush

page 18—Film Grain

page 20—Fresco

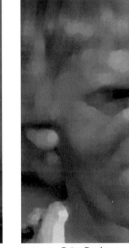
page 22—Neon Glow

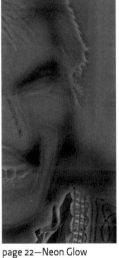
page 24—Paint Daubs

page 28—Plastic Wrap

page 30—Poster Edges

page 32—Rough Pastels

page 34—Smudge Stick

page 36—Underpainting

page 37—Watercolor

Palette Knife

The Palette Knife filter works by approximating colors in patches across the image, simplifying detail in a pattern reminiscent of the Crystallize filter (see page 106). The size of these patches is controlled by the Stroke Size slider. Unlike Crystallize, there is some color bleeding between adjacent patches. We'll look at one technique here which adds the missing tactile qualities.

How it works

1 At Stroke Size 5, Stroke Detail 3, and Softness 5, the portrait image is scarcely affected. The result can be seen in close-up.

2 Increasing the Stroke size to 10 brings strong blacks into the shadow areas.

3 The same settings applied to the target image yield somewhat better results.

(see page 106)

Using the Palette Knife filter

1 A straightforward application of the Palette Knife filter at Stroke Size 17, Stroke Detail 3, Softness 1 softens the image, but there's no sign of the tactile qualities that a real palette knife would add.

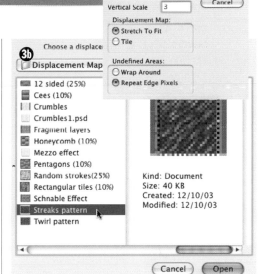

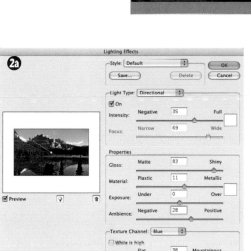

2a, 2b Go to Filter > Render > Lighting Effects, and use the values shown here— select Directional light, increase the Shiny value in Properties, select the existing image's blue channel as the Texture channel, and hit OK. What we're trying to achieve here is to keep a similar tonal quality to the image, but to add more of a 3D effect, and give the image some depth.

3a, 3b Some diligent work with the Smudge tool might be beneficial here. A quicker alternative is to go to **Filter > Distort > Displace**, choosing the greater distortion figure in the horizontal axis, and selecting Streaks Pattern from the default Photoshop Displacement Maps folder (this folder should be in the Plug-Ins folder in the main application folder). The amount of distortion required depends on the size of the image, so you might need to try a few different settings before finding something that works.

4 The result may not be great art, but it does give a certain painterly quality to the photograph.

Colored Pencil

The Colored Pencil filter aims to imitate a diagonally cross-hatched pencil sketch, the effect centering around significant edges in the image. Use the Pencil Width slider at low values for more a detailed appearance. Stroke Pressure controls the amount of cross-hatching. With the default white as the background color in the color palette, the background "paper color" will first appear as 50% gray. Move the Paper Brightness slider to the left to approach solid black, and to the right for pure white. Change the default white to any other color before using the filter; the selected color will then become the paper color. Use the Paper Brightness slider to control its intensity.

How it works

1 The Pencil Width, Stroke Pressure, and Paper Brightness sliders are at 1, 10, and 25 respectively.

2 Only the Stroke Pressure is increased slightly, to 15. The effect is to retain more of the original image.

3 The close-up view shows the opposing groups of strokes in greater detail.

4 Increasing the value of Pencil Width to 5 produces a more graphic effect.

5 Keeping the same Pencil Width, but reducing Stroke Pressure to 5 while increasing Paper Brightness to 30 lets the background show through.

6 A further increase in Paper Brightness to 45 produces a more "drawn" effect.

7 Keeping the high Paper Brightness and increasing the Pencil Width to 20 finally pushes the image off the useful scale.

8a, 8b These two images show the importance of image resolution with this and many other filters that aim for a linear effect. The first is at 300ppi, the conventional resolution for commercial printing, while the second, although the same physical size, is only at 72ppi—the norm for screen display. In the latter, there are simply not enough pixels available to produce the desired effect.

9 Here, you can see the result of changing the palette background color to bright blue (changing the foreground color has no effect on this filter).

10 Our target image offers too few strong tonal shifts in the background, producing only a few half-hearted strokes.

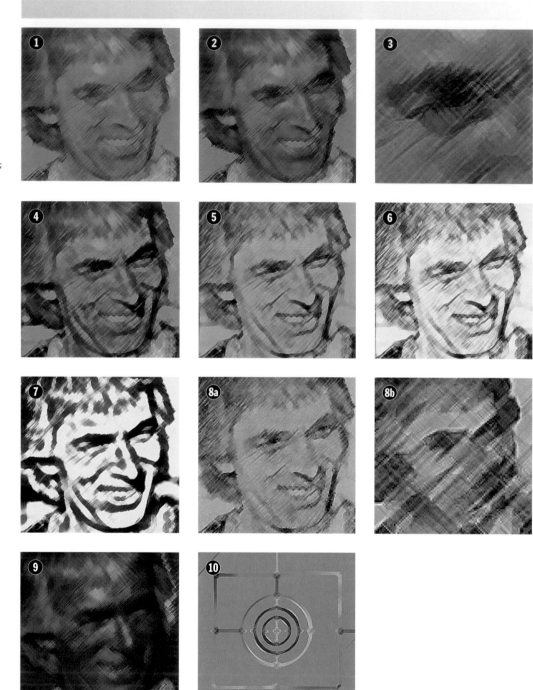

One way of getting a better effect from this filter is to apply it to two separate layers, and then merge the two using blending modes.

1 To make a more intense mesh of "pencil" lines, start by duplicating the source image—click and drag its thumbnail over the "turned page" icon at the foot of the Layers palette.

2 Choose the Eyedropper tool from the Tools palette and click in the source image to establish a background "paper color." Here, we have picked up a light brown from the wooden decking.

3 You can of course choose any background you wish, but choosing a color from within the image leads to a more harmonious result. In the Tools palette, click on the curved arrow next to the foreground/background swatches to set the newly selected color as the background color.

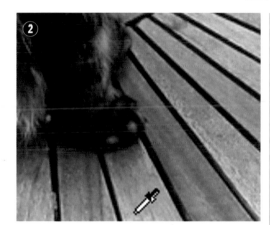

4 Run the Colored Pencil filter, varying the Paper Brightness slider carefully to control the overall effect. We've chosen a tone that's very similar to the original background color, but do experiment with the slider.

5a, 5b Re-duplicate the source layer and run the filter again, using the same settings (Ctrl/Cmd+F) or by reselecting the Colored Pencil filter and adjusting the settings as you wish. Return to the Layers palette and change the blending mode and opacity of the topmost layer to visually merge the two layers. Experiment to find the best result—there are many possibilities, some of which are immediately and obviously unsuitable. Here, we've used Linear Light at 50% opacity.

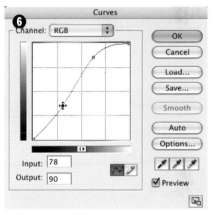

6 The result can be improved further by applying **Image > Adjustments > Curves** to both layers to alter the tonal range. Here, we've increased the intensity of the midtones and shadows to give a little more strength to the image.

7 The final step is to erase the eyes in both Colored Pencil layers, returning some personality to the subject and providing a natural focal point for the image.

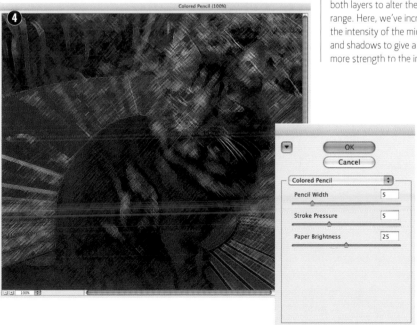

Cutout

The Cutout filter reduces the number of colors in an image by approximating similar and adjacent colors into areas resembling cut-out pieces of paper. The Number of Levels slider controls the number of colors, while Edge Simplicity makes the "cut" edges more, or less, complex. The related Edge Fidelity slider determines how closely the edges follow the shapes in the original image. Additionally, try using the Lighting Effects filter (see page 118) to enhance the initial result of Cutout. You can simulate shadows cast by the individual fragments by choosing one of the RGB channels as a texture channel.

How it works

1 When you set the number of levels, Photoshop looks for similar colors and groups them. The effect superficially resembles that produced by the Posterize function in the **Image > Adjustments** menu.

2a, 2b, 2c With Edge Simplicity and Fidelity at minimum, progressive increases in Levels produce a more "realistic" effect. Subtleties in the original (note the receding hairline in 2a) are suppressed at lower Level settings.

3a, 3b Edge Simplicity is a very blunt instrument. The facial features are still just about recognizable at a setting of 4, but an increase of just two points begins to break the image into much more jagged planes.

4a, 4b Edge Fidelity restores some of the integrity of the original. Compare 4a and 4b: the second image has Edge Fidelity increased to 3, the maximum, so that slight, but vital, detail is retained.

5 With all sliders set to minimum, the target is reduced to six colors.

6a, 6b Images 6a and 6b show the effect on the target of minimum and maximum Edge Fidelity settings respectively.

7 This filter works equally well on monochrome subjects. Compare this result with the original color version at the same filter settings in step 3. Once you have the image in this form, you can return to color mode and transform the levels of gray into your own choice of colors.

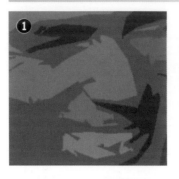

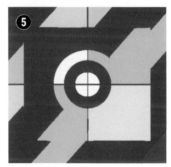

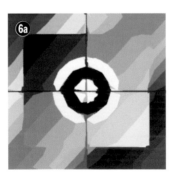

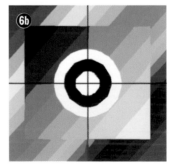

This effect mimics the style of the large-format posters of 1920-1950, produced mostly by the silkscreen process. Flat colors and simplified shapes were the norm, relieved by areas of overlap made with thinned layers of ink.

The most important decision to be made when using this filter is picture selection. Complex details don't react well to it, and portraits often look bizarre.

In addition, it may be necessary to modify all or parts of the image before applying filters to achieve the desired result. Once the basic effect has been established, there are further possibilities: changing color values area by area or globally; repeating the simplification process; re-tracing the newly formed edges, or amending the image by hand or with the History Brush.

1 The selected image contains bold shapes, a strong composition, and plenty of contrast. The high viewpoint and extreme wide-angle view (18mm lens equivalent) produces diverging verticals—note the tree and the utility pole—but here they contribute to the dynamics of the picture.

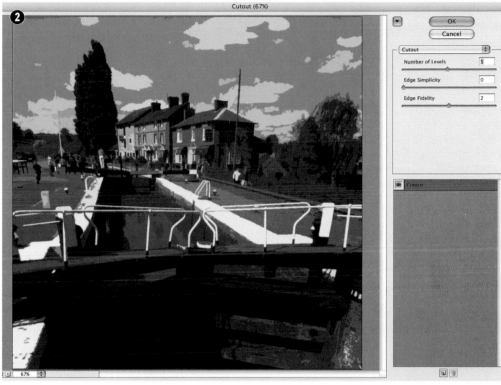

2 Edge Simplicity would have been a more intuitive control if labeled Edge Complexity and arranged to run in the opposite direction. In any case, for this effect we need a detailed edge, so the slider is set to zero. The other controls are centered for now. The initial result is mostly satisfactory, with exception of the rather flat hedge on the right of the towpath. Other areas, notably the tall fir tree, have obligingly mutated into a silkscreen style.

3 To add more variation to the flat area, choose the Lasso tool at a fairly large feather. The actual amount will depend on the pixel dimensions of the original image (this one is around 1100 pixels wide).

4 Great accuracy isn't required here, so make a rough selection of the desired area.

ARTISTIC
Cutout

5 Check that your color palette is set to the default black and white, and choose **Filter > Render > Clouds**. The initial result doesn't look very promising.

6 Now go to **Edit > Fade Clouds** and select Overlay as the blending mode. This maneuver adds some contrast and tonal variation.

7 When you deselect the lassoed area and reapply the original Cutout setting, the disturbance caused is enough to generate more complex shapes, which match the rest of the filtered image.

8 If you increase the number of levels, the image will tend to revert to a more "photographic" appearance. In this example, the Levels setting has been increased to the maximum.

9 Alternatively, you can increase the Edge Simplicity to 2, to produce a much more blocky result.

Sponge

In the same vein as the Film Grain and Smudge Stick filters, Sponge applies a random pattern to an image that can be clearly seen by using it on a plain area of 50% gray. Use it in moderation to add emphasis to an existing crumbly texture, or as a junior partner in combination with other filters, as can be seen in the following example.

How it works

1 At these initially low settings of Brush Size 3, Definition 3, Smoothness 1, the Sponge filter strongly resembles its neighbor in the Artistic suite, the Smudge Stick filter.

2 At higher settings (8, 13, 5), the pattern behind the filter becomes more obtrusive.

3 The target image is softened and textured with settings of 0, 25, and 15.

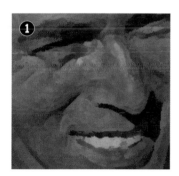

Using the Sponge filter

This rather circuitous technique sidesteps the deadening effect of the Sponge filter when it is applied conventionally.

1 The aim is to boost the watery quality of this image and give it an element of faux-3D.

2 Apply the Sponge filter at Brush size 6, Definition 16, Smoothness 10, and the characteristic gray mottling will instantly appear.

3 Select all (Ctrl/Cmd+A) and copy (Ctrl/Cmd+C), then create a new Photoshop document. The dialog box will open with the dimensions and resolution of the document you just copied. Give it a suitable name and choose Grayscale as the Color Mode.

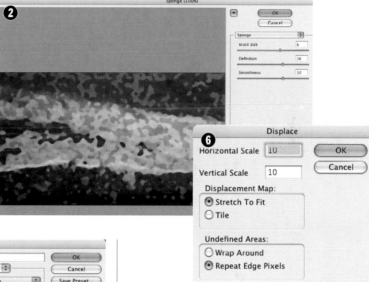

6. Choose **Filter > Distort > Displace**, using the preset values. Hit OK.

7 When the Open dialog appears, select the grayscale document you made before (you'll find it where it was saved) and click Open.

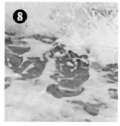

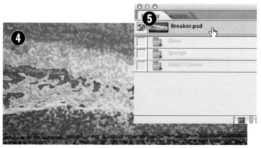

4 Paste in the breaker image, then flatten the image (click on the button at top right of the Layers palette to find the command), save it as a full Photoshop document, and then close it.

5 Return to the main document and use the History palette to return it to its original, unfiltered state. If the History palette is not available, you'll find it under the Window menu.

8 The result escapes the murky mottling, and in close-up it shows the development of interesting forms. To enhance the effect, repeat this step by reselecting **Filter > Displace** (or Ctrl/Cmd+F).

Dry Brush

The Dry Brush filter produces a stippled appearance on a raised-contrast version of the original image. The Brush Size slider controls the number of distinct color areas, while increasing values of Brush Detail reduce the amount of pixelation at the color boundaries. The three levels of Texture progressively add contrast, thus emphasizing the edge pixelation. Although the effect isn't much like a real paintbrush, this filter can be useful for breaking images into pools of color, but with a less harsh effect than Cutout. Use the Edit > Fade command after applying the filter to help blend it with the original image.

How it works

1a–d Increasing Brush Size progressively obscures the original image, finally producing an unacceptably macabre result.

2 With the filter sliders set at 10, 10, and 3, a partially painterly result is achieved. See page 37 for examples of similar effects using the Watercolor filter.

3a–d The Texture slider introduces a mottled artefact at medium (3a) and maximum (3b) settings. A magnification (3c) shows the curious "brush" pattern at pixel size, and also a spurious edge effect at the left side (3d).

4 With settings at minimum (4a), fine lines in the target are still preserved. At maximum settings (4b), Brush Size overcomes Brush Detail, producing a flat result.

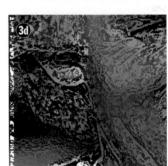

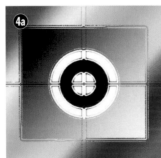
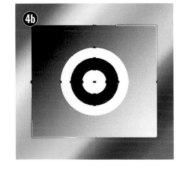

Dry Brush works well on architectural subjects. This example uses the Pen tool to isolate areas for differing treatments in imitation of a partially finished artwork.

1 Make sure that the Pen tool is set to create paths in the Options bar, then click around the perimeter of the chosen area until the path is complete. If you now check the Paths palette, your path should appear as Work Path.

2a, 2b The button at the top right of the Paths palette gives access to a sub-menu. Choose Make Selection to bring up the dialog box of the same name. You may find that anti-aliasing the path with a small Feather helps to round any sharp edges in the resulting selection and better blend it with the original image.

3 Run the Dry Brush filter on the selection, with a medium Brush Size, high Brush Detail, and minimum Texture setting.
To work with the rest of the image, inverse the selection by pressing Ctrl/Cmd+Shift+I or going to Select > Inverse.

4 To affect the color level in the background area, choose Image > Adjustments > Hue/Saturation. Check the Colorize box to eliminate local color present in the original, drag the Saturation slider to a low level, and Increase the Lightness value. Move the Hue slider to establish a suitable color to imitate the qualities of a pencil sketch.

5 The result is shown with the gray work area exposed to illustrate the full extent of the selection.

6 Keeping the same selection, use Filter > Noise > Add Noise and the settings shown to add texture to the image.

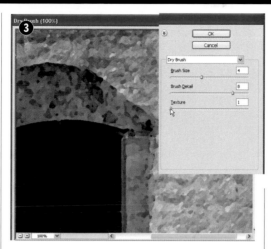

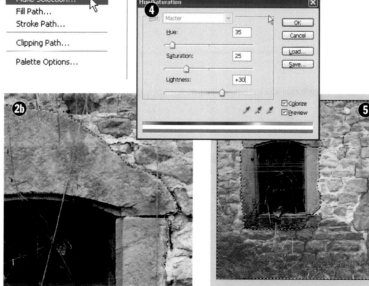

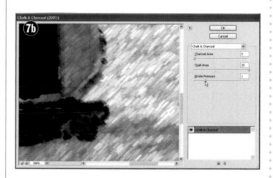

7a, 7b Change the foreground palette color to the dominant color by clicking the Eyedropper tool in a dark area. You can also choose a new "paper" color by clicking in the background color palette and selecting a light tint. Finally, go to **Filter > Sketch > Chalk & Charcoal** for the result.

8 The finished effect is painterly, but with a strong focal point. You can develop the exercise further by selecting smaller areas of the image and using other filters, such as Graphic Pen and Conté Crayon to enhance the "drawn" image

17

Film Grain

eal film grain forms in clumps according to the amount of light falling on the emulsion. A powerful magnification of the transition between a light and dark area shows the change in pattern. Photoshop's Film Grain filter, however, is a random pattern—it doesn't react directly to light or dark areas in the subject—and compromises by applying a different texture to the light tones than it does to the middle and dark tones. This function is controlled by the Highlight Area and Intensity sliders. You can use this filter to "roughen up" components in montages which look too well-defined in comparison with their neighbors, though this can be done in a more controlled way using the various filters in the Noise suite.

How it works

1 The Highlight Area and Intensity sliders determine the extent of the grain pattern. The Grain control adds more or less grain within the defined areas.

This is another filter where image resolution is important, with the filter having a much more destructive effect on lower resolution images.

2 With maximum Grain selected, but both Highlight Area and Intensity set to

zero, the image is almost obscured by the over-abundance of noise.

3 If you stay with maximum Grain, but insert a high value for Highlight Area and a moderate setting for Intensity, you'll get a result which begins to approximate an over-exposed color print with accentuated grain.

4 And, just for the record, here's the target image at medium settings.

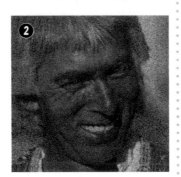

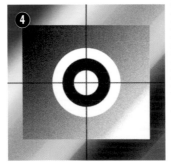

In digital photography, we are beset by square pixels and noise that arrives in unpleasant rectangular chunks, so there's nothing more natural than to yearn for the organic harmonies of good old-fashioned film grain. Technicians in white coats disappoint, however, by reminding us that the objects of our affection were not grains at all. Individual film grains, more properly "filaments," are only revealed at magnifications of 30 times and above. The speckles that we're after are clumps of many filaments, and that is one reason why the Photoshop filter is only an approximation of the real thing. In color transparency film, for example, the speckles occur in three constituent layers—yellow, magenta, and cyan. Unlike the four-color printing process, there is no black element. The following technique attempts to imitate the structure of a film transparency by manipulating the individual color channels in Photoshop.

1a, 1b The original image is an RGB file with three channels, which can be seen in the Channels palette. However, instead of RGB, we require CMY.

2a, 2b The first step is to change to the four channels of CMYK. This can be done from the Image menu. The Channels palette reflects this with four elements, and it might seem a good opportunity to discard the black channel by clicking on it and dragging it to the trash can icon at the bottom of the palette.

3 The result, however, is clearly disastrous.

4 Revert to the full CMYK image, and duplicate it in the Layers palette by dragging the thumbnail onto the turned-page icon at the foot of the palette. In the Channels palette, select the Cyan channel, call up the Mezzotint filter (**Filter > Pixelate > Mezzotint**) and choose Fine Dots.

5 Fade the Mezzotint filter using Vivid Light by selecting **Edit > Fade Mezzotint**, and choosing Vivid Light as the blending mode.

6 Repeat this operation on the two remaining color channels, but don't treat the black channel. You can view the cumulative effect by clicking on the eyeball icon of the relevant channels.

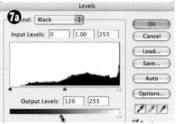

TIP

Channel thumbnails in a Photoshop file display in tones of gray by default. Go to Preferences > Display and Cursors and check Color Channels in Color to work with them more easily.

7a, 7b The black channel is overly dominant, so treat it with **Image > Adjustments > Levels** to tone it down.

8 The result lacks structure, so return to the Layers palette and change the blending mode to Pin Light to restore some of the values of the underlying layer.

9 Other variations are easily achieved. For example, when running Mezzotint here, we've used Long Lines rather than Fine Dots for the type.

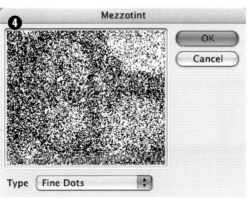

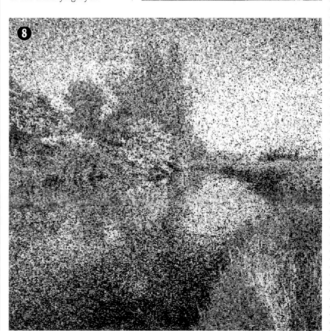

Fresco

The Fresco filter is a close cousin of the Dry Brush filter, and similarly looks little like its real-life counterpart. It adds a black overlay to existing shadow areas, leaving highlight areas untouched. The Texture slider adds a gray pixel pattern.

Real fresco involves covering a wall with a smooth coat of plaster, and applying paint while the plaster is still wet, or at least damp, to the touch. Any dry, unpainted areas have to be hacked out before the next painting session can begin. In this regard, the Fresco filter is less laborious than the real thing.

How it works

1 Three sliders control Brush Size, Brush Detail, and Texture. The last slider can profitably be left set at 1, using the others to obtain watercolor-like effects.

2 Brush Size 0 and Brush Detail at maximum 10 gives a mottled result.

3 Using maximum Brush Size and minimum Detail offers a broad-brush effect that is probably the closest to real fresco.

4 With the same settings, the target image loses its fine lines and gains some diagonal brushstrokes.

Using the Fresco filter

We'll use a close-up of some painted wallpaper to stand in for a newly frescoed Florentine wall.

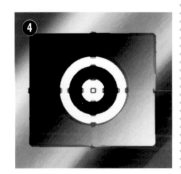

1 This portrait of a young woman is copied and pasted as a new layer in our wallpaper image.

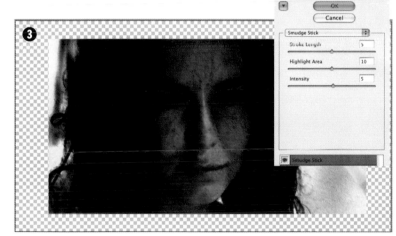

2 Change the blending mode to Hard Light to give the impression that the face has merged with the wall.

3 Next, run the Smudge Stick filter with settings of Stroke Length 5, Highlight Area 10, and Intensity 5 on the newly pasted image.

4 Follow this up with the Fresco filter set to Brush Size 2, Brush Detail 1, and Texture 2, faded to around 40% in Pin Light mode.

5 You can fine-tune the show-through of the wall component at this stage by reducing the Face layer's opacity. We settled for 60%, for a more convincing result. Not exactly Piero della Francesca, but close.

Neon Glow

Neon Glow is the first filter in the Artistic suite to require a two-step approach. Leaving the default black/white palette as it is, the whole image, bar the highlights, is reduced to gray. The Glow Color panel gives access to the Color Picker where you can choose a color to influence the highlights. For more interesting effects, change the foreground color before using the filter. The gray image will be colorized following your color choice. In the filter dialog box, select a contrasting glow color for the highlights. Experiment by choosing similar colors for foreground and glow—you can then concentrate on manipulating the highlight values.

How it works

1 Begin by leaving the default black and white palette and selecting a color in the filter dialog box. The possibilities are rather restricted, ranging from a slight glow to a bizarre quasi-negative effect.

2 Here, the settings are Glow Size 9, Glow Brightness 14, and a purple for the Glow Color.

3 With bright blue selected as the foreground color, more extreme results can be expected. A third color can be brought into play by selecting a new background color. This newly introduced color merges with the Glow Color that's selected in the filter dialog box.

4 The same settings turn the target image to mud.

Using the Neon Glow filter

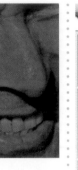

1 To produce the illusion of internal lighting with this alphabet example, you need to first change the default foreground color in the Tools palette. Here we've chosen a baby blue.

2 It's useful at this stage to measure the width of the letters in pixels. The easiest way to do this is to use the Measure tool. Click and hold the mouse on the Eyedropper tool in the Toolbox to reveal it. Click and drag across one of the letters, and the distance will appear in the Options Bar. Another method is to simply use the Rectangular Marquee tool. With the Info window open (if it's not visible, go to the main menu and look in the Window submenu) click and drag a selection box across a letter. The pixel width will appear in the bottom right corner of the Info window— 76 pixels in this case. If you prefer to work in other units, you can access them by clicking on the arrow at the top right of the window.

3 Next, click on the Magic Wand tool. Settings for the Magic Wand will appear in the Options Bar.

7a, 7b To confine the selection to the central area of each letter, go to **Select > Modify > Contract** and insert a suitable value. Since the letter is 76 pixels wide, inserting a value of 20 pixels will select around half its width (that is, it will subtract 20 pixels from each side).

8 To soften the selection, go to **Select > Modify > Feather**—we've used a value of 15 pixels.

4 Choose the first of the four options in the Selection type palette, increase the tolerance and, if necessary, uncheck Contiguous. The wand will now select all similar colors wherever they occur in the image—with Contiguous checked, it will only select an individual area. In close-up you can see that the set tolerance was too small and has not selected all the blue areas.

5 You could track back a stage and increase the tolerance, but it's easier just to Shift-click in the offending area with the Magic Wand. All similar areas will be brought into the selection.

6 Keep Shift held down and click in the orange area, for example, and continue in this way until all the letter forms have been selected.

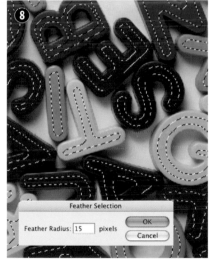

9 With this selection active, choose the Neon Glow filter with a Glow Size of 14, a Glow Brightness of 50 and a blue Glow Color.

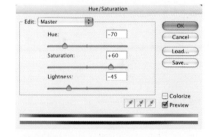

NEON GLOW VARIATION

For a simple variation, keep the selection active, go to Select > Inverse to choose the previously unselected areas, and use Image > Adjustments > Hue/Saturation to change all three values to your desired result.

23

Paint Daubs

Paint Daubs simulates a broad brush charged with a single color per stroke. With this filter you can select from a range of brush styles; Paint Daubs offers a range from (a) comic-book lithograph (Brush Size 2, Sharpness 40, Simple brush) to (b) virtuoso oil painting (Brush Size 25, Sharpness 8, Wide Sharp brush). The most useful brushes are Simple and Wide Blurry. The remainder—Light Rough, Dark Rough, Wide Sharp, and Sparkle—introduce a distracting veil of spectral colors at most settings.

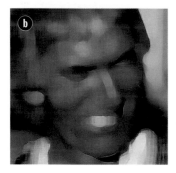

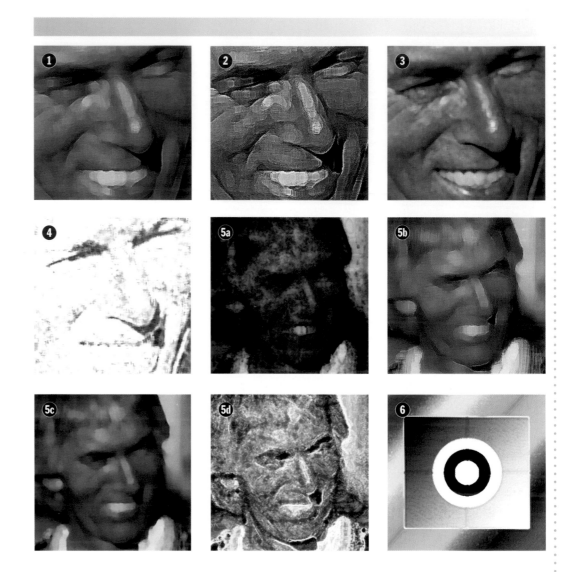

How it works

1 A soft effect can be best achieved with the Simple brush at minimum Brush Size and low Sharpness (10 and 8 in this case).

2 Setting Sharpness to maximum (40) gives more contrast, introducing sharp lines in the shadow areas.

3 With the Light Rough brush selected, minimum Brush Size and Sharpness are once again the most useful settings.

4 With only medium Sharpness, the image is almost completely blown out. The same is true for the Dark Rough and Wide Sharp brush settings.

5a–d The rogue's gallery: Light Rough (5a), Wide Sharp (5b), Wide Blurry (5c) and Sparkle (5d) all at their least offensive settings.

6 The target image loses its fine lines and develops round shoulders with the Simple brush and both sliders at medium settings.

24

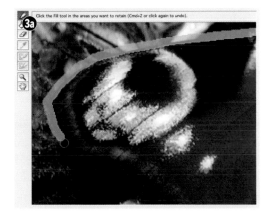

Shot "on the fly" with no preparation, this image, though acceptably sharp and with good color saturation, suffers from a confusing background and flat flash lighting. On the plus side, it already has some of the qualities of an artistic rendering. Using Paint Daubs as the primary filter, it can be transformed into an image with more painterly qualities.

1 It's always a good idea to duplicate your original image (click and drag the original image layer thumbnail down on to the "turned page" icon at the foot of the palette) before making any serious adjustments. Next, use the Crop tool to remove surplus areas of the image.

2 The next stage is to lift the butterfly from its background. There are several routes from which to choose: Extract in the filter menu; Magic Wand or Eraser from the toolbox; or simply using the Lasso tool to select the required area. Extract and Magic Wand work best when there are distinct color and/or tonal differences between wanted and unwanted areas, but the latter in particular requires lengthy cleaning up afterwards. The Lasso tool's effectiveness is only limited by your persistence in clicking around the profile of the chosen image, but is of limited use when the object has an indistinct outline or, in the worst case, flyaway hair. In this example, I'm going to use a combination of Extract and the History State/History Brush. Go to **Filter > Extract**. The dialog box that appears offers a number of options for setting the parameters of the extraction.

3a, 3b Choose a small brush, and select Textured Image with a medium Smoothing factor. The idea is to draw as closely as possible around the area to be extracted, using the I lighlighter tool at the top of the palette, keeping the desired edge in the center of the selection. You can change the brush width to a smaller size to work in more detailed areas.

Paint Daubs

Click Preview to see the image with the background removed or OK to extract and exit immediately.

4a, 4b With the outline complete, it's finally time to use the Paint Bucket tool to fill it. This serves to tell the filter which area you wish to retain, and the result of your labors is clear to see when you click Preview.

5 You can further finesse the edge with the Edge Touchup tool, and its near neighbor in the palette, the Cleanup tool. You'll need to reselect the Highlighter tool, refill with the Paint Bucket and click Preview again to see the result.

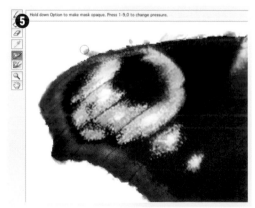

Click OK to apply results or Use Cleanup, Edge Touchup tools to modify results.

Hold down Option to make mask opaque. Press 1-9,0 to change pressure.

6 Another line of attack is to use the Eraser tool on the highlighter line to adjust the shape of the selection.

7a, 7b When all seems satisfactory, refill the central area, click Preview and then OK to return to the layered image. Run Paint Daubs on the cut-out image with these settings: Brush Size 2, Sharpness 2, Brush Type Wide Blurry. Follow this with the Watercolor filter set to Brush Detail 11, Shadow Intensity 0, and Texture 1.

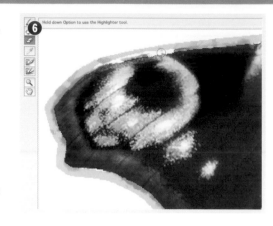

Hold down Option to use the Highlighter tool.

Paint Daubs (100%)

7a

Paint Daubs

Brush Size — 2
Sharpness — 2
Brush Type: Wide Blurry

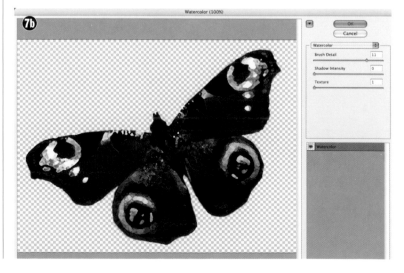

Watercolor (100%)

7b

Watercolor

Brush Detail — 11
Shadow Intensity — 0
Texture — 1

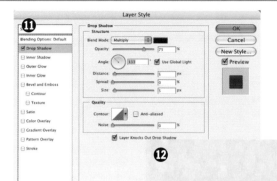

8 To limit the overly aggressive effect of this filter, immediately invoke **Edit > Fade Watercolor** and choose Screen at 50% opacity. The result is a compromise between the original photograph and an artistic rendering.

9a, 9b To generate an instant background, click on the "Create new layer" icon and fill the new layer with a straw color. Next run **Filter > Render > Fibers**.

10 Apply the Blur, Add Noise, and Paint Daubs filters to this layer until it begins to soften and retreat into semi-obscurity.

11 Returning to the butterfly layer, try the various effects available in the **Layer > Layer Style** menu (accessible also through the tiny button marked with an italic "f" at the foot of the layer thumbnails palette).

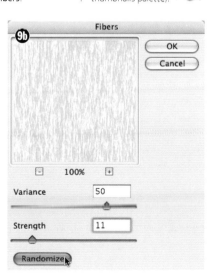

12 Here, we've added a drop shadow, but the "airbrush" effect of the default settings doesn't sit well with the painterly qualities of the rest of the image.

13 The effect of the drop shadow can be altered in the Layer Style dialog.

14 Here, the shadow color has been changed to brown, and its Contour altered to break up the shadow's shape. You can also add Noise in the same window to blend in the shadow—the result, in close-up, is a less strident shadow.

15 Flatten the layers to see the final result.

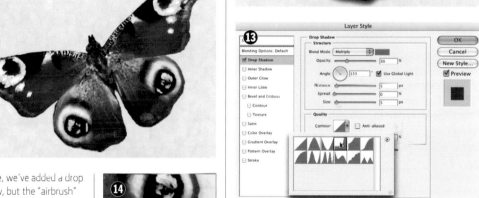

27

Plastic Wrap

Plastic Wrap introduces monochrome highlight and shadows in darker image areas. The "blister pack" illusion of peaks and troughs is due to the built-in lighting plot, revealed by applying the filter to a plain black area. Plastic Wrap is generally used in conjunction with other filters and Layer blends (see page 29, for example) and it works rather better on inanimate objects than on things that really shouldn't be shrink-wrapped in real life.

How it works

1 The dialog offers three controls: Highlight Strength, Detail, and Smoothness. Setting all three at high levels (16, 12, and 12 respectively) gives the classic "blister pack" appearance.

2 Lower levels of Highlight Strength give the illusion of the subject protruding through the "plastic" layer. The other two controls are at maximum value.

3 The effect on the inanimate target image is clearly less disturbing than on a human face.

Applying the filter to a pure black background clearly shows the lighting mechanism at work.

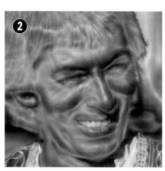

4a- 4c Unsurprisingly, Plastic Wrap is ideally suited to vegetables. This shrink-wrapped market stall is ready to be delivered direct to the supermarket.

Highlight Strength	17
Detail	12
Smoothness	11

28

This classic example of the extra-long-exposure moving-water shot lends itself to a little selective shrink-wrapping.

1 First set the Marquee tool to a larger Feather value to make a soft selection. As a guide, this picture is about 1700 pixels wide, and the feather selection is a little under one-tenth of that amount.

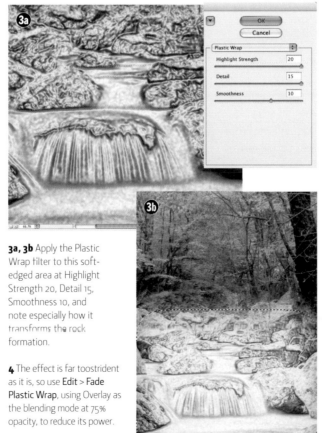

1

| | | Feather: 125 px | Anti-alias | Style: Normal |

2a, 2b Drag on the lower right corner of the document window to reveal the gray work area surrounding the image. This makes it easier to select the target area accurately, by starting the click and drag in the gray and then continuing right across the image to select the whole waterfall.

RGB/8)

Fade

Opacity: 75 % OK
Cancel
Mode: Overlay ☑ Preview

5 Deselect the marquee and run the Plastic Wrap filter again—just hit Ctrl/Cmd+F— but this time apply it to the whole image, so that the lower area gets a double dose of the filter.

6 More fading is required. Immediately go to **Edit > Fade Plastic Wrap** once again, but this time use Pin Light at about 50% opacity for the final touch.

OK
Cancel

Plastic Wrap

Highlight Strength   20

Detail   15

Smoothness   10

3a, 3b Apply the Plastic Wrap filter to this soft-edged area at Highlight Strength 20, Detail 15, Smoothness 10, and note especially how it transforms the rock formation.

4 The effect is far too strident as it is, so use **Edit > Fade Plastic Wrap**, using Overlay as the blending mode at 75% opacity, to reduce its power.

Fade

Opacity: 50 % OK
Cancel
Mode: Pin Light ☑ Preview

16.67%   Doc: 11.6M/11.6M

Poster Edges

With care, you can use this filter to achieve echoes of old-style cinema posters and lobby cards. It's not to be confused with Posterization (in the Image > Adjustments menu), Poster Edges has a more sedate effect. Edge Thickness and Edge Intensity control the production of black lines at existing contrast boundaries in the image. The Posterization slider works independently on a scale from 0 (maximum effect) to 6 (little effect).

How it works

1 At settings: Edge Thickness 0, Edge Intensity 0, Posterization 6, the only discernible difference in this image is a thickening of the shadow areas. Compare this to the original (see below).

2a, 2b There is also little difference between the image treated at medium levels with all three controls— Edge Thickness 5, Edge Intensity 5, Posterization 3— and that made with low Edge Thickness (set to 1) and a high degree of Posterization (set to 6).

3 At the same settings of Edge Thickness 1, Edge Intensity 5, and Posterization 6, the target image shows accentuated edges but little or no change to the graduated areas.

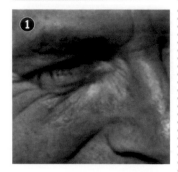

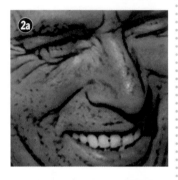

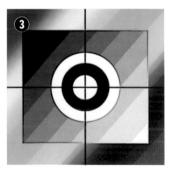

Using the Poster Edges filter

Image selection is the key to success with Poster Edges. Look for strong contrast and plenty of edge detail.

This whisky distillery obliges with lots of regular and irregular forms for the filter to bite on.

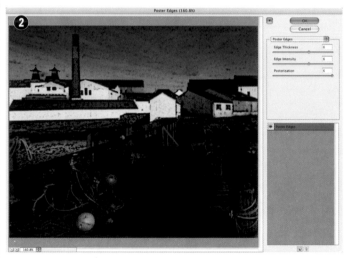

1a, 1b Duplicate the original layer and click on the Background eyeball in the Layers palette to make that layer invisible.

2 Run Poster Edges at medium intensity—Edge Thickness 6, Edge Intensity 6, Posterization 6. The Posterization slider is not directly significant for this technique, but changing its value does have a marginal effect on the production of a strong black line. The initial effect is disappointingly dark, but there are some interesting changes in the brighter areas of the image.

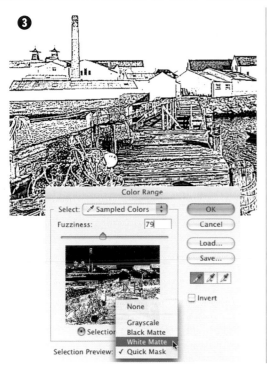

❸

Color Range

Select: ✎ Sampled Colors ⌄

Fuzziness: 79

OK
Cancel
Load...
Save...

☐ Invert

◉ Selection

Selection Preview: ✓ Quick Mask

None
Grayscale
Black Matte
White Matte
✓ Quick Mask

❻

Channels | Paths

Normal ⌄ | Opacity:

Lock: ☐ ✎ ✦ | Fill:

Background copy

Background

6 Unlock the background layer by double-clicking on its layer thumbnail and hitting OK when the dialog window appears.

7 Use Filter > Artistic > Cutout to reduce the number of colors, but choose the maximum number of levels, with the minimum Edge Simplicity, and maximum Edge Fidelity.

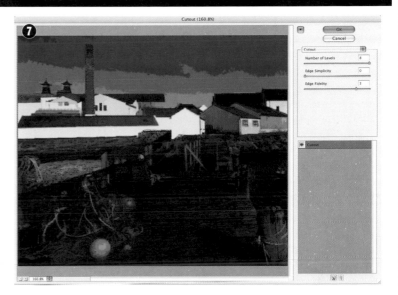

Cutout (160.8%)

❼

OK
Cancel

Cutout

Number of Levels   8
Edge Simplicity   0
Edge Fidelity   3

Cutout

8 Now make the upper layer visible to see the combined effect of the filters.

3 With black selected as the default foreground color (if it isn't, just hit D on the keyboard), go to Select > Color Range and move the slider left and right to get the best result. Choose White Matte as the Selection Preview. When you're satisfied, hit OK.

❹

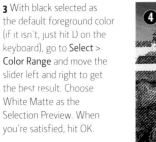

❽

❾

Tolerance: 8   ☑ Anti-alias

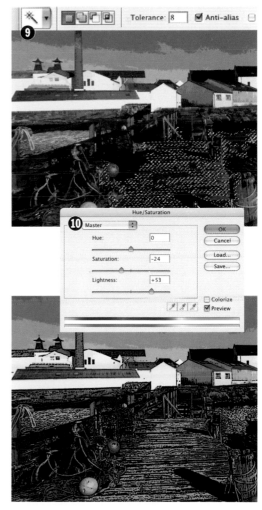

4 The preview disappears and the "marching ants" denote the selected areas.

5 Invert the selection (Ctrl/Cmd+Shift+I) and hit Backspace or choose Edit > Clear. What remains is just the black line component. Deselect (Ctrl/Cmd+D).

❺

9 Staying in the treated cutout layer, it's easy to select individual colors for amendment using the Magic Wand tool set to a small tolerance (with Contiguous unchecked). Add other colors to the selection by holding down Shift (you'll see a + sign underneath the magic wand icon).

10 Treat the selected colors with Image > Adjustments > Hue/Saturation. In this case, the foreground timber deck area benefits greatly from lightening and desaturation.

Hue/Saturation

❿ Master ⌄

Hue: 0
Saturation: -24
Lightness: +53

OK
Cancel
Load...
Save...

☐ Colorize
☑ Preview

Rough Pastels

Traditionally, the pastel technique is generally associated with soft effects on a light-colored ground, but the great masters of pastel also used the dramatic contrast of light marks on a dark ground. This filter operates more on the texture than the color of an image, but with the right source it can give interesting results. With four sliders, two pop-up menus offering a total of 12 options, and an Invert function, there are thousands of combinations for this filter. This calculation ignores the use of the Load Texture function, accessed via the fly-out button, that allows you to introduce other textured grounds. Note that the Relief slider in the Texture section must have a value—otherwise the pastel effect won't appear.

How it works

1 The pastel itself, always appearing diagonally across the screen, is controlled by the Stroke Length and Stroke Detail sliders. The "working surface" (set to Canvas by default) has controls for Texture type, Scaling, Relief, and Light Direction. Moving the Relief control toward zero diminishes the pastel effect.

2 This effect was achieved with Stroke Length 9, Stroke Detail 11, Scaling 150, and Relief 50, with light coming from top right.

3 To get just a slight pastel effect, choose minimum Stroke Length, low Stroke Detail, 50% Scaling, and a low value for Relief.

4a, 4b For a more emphatic result, increase both Stroke Length and Stroke Detail to 15, Scaling to 100%, and Relief to 20. Different textures at the same settings give quite different results.

5 The monochrome image shows a discreet effect with low levels for all sliders— Stroke Length 0, Stroke Detail 5, Scaling 50, and Relief 25. This chalk and charcoal effect can be further developed with the dedicated Chalk & Charcoal filter in the Sketch menu (see page 132).

6 At the same settings, the target image reveals part of the mechanism behind the filter—edges are displaced then eroded with the background texture.

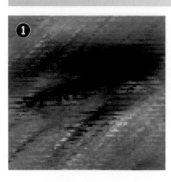

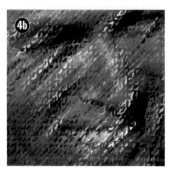

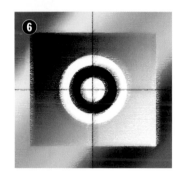

Although the Rough Pastels filter is generally too strong to be left as is, a combination of carefully selected blending modes and lowered opacity can add dynamism to flat original photographs.

1 This very underexposed shot of patriotic British concert-goers provides a good starting point for a simple maneuver.

2 Duplicate the original image in the Layers palette by dragging its thumbnail onto the turned-page icon. Repeat this to make a total of three layers.

3 Select the top layer and apply the Rough Pastels filter with all sliders pushed to maximum. Following artistic tradition, set the Light Direction to Top Left and leave Texture on the default Canvas setting.

4 The initial effect is extreme, but don't despair.

5 Turn off visibility on the treated layer (click on the eyeball icon) and activate the second layer. Select all (Ctrl/Cmd+A), go to **Image > Rotate Canvas > Flip Canvas Horizontal** and apply the filter again at the same settings (Ctrl/Cmd+F). Repeat the Flip Canvas Horizontal command to bring the image back to its original orientation.

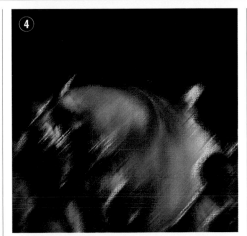

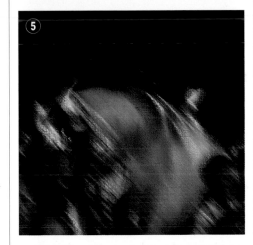

6 The result of the flipping is that we now have pastel marks running in both directions. We now need to alter the blending mode of the top layer to reveal the layer below.

Click in the top layer thumbnail to activate it. Change the blending mode to Screen and the opacity to 60%. Repeat this change for the second layer.

7 The reduction in opacity in the top two layers allows a little of the original photographic structure to show through, and the bidirectional stroke pattern lends an additional dynamic.

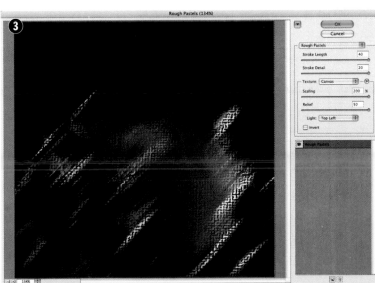

Smudge Stick

Try Smudge Stick for smearing pixels in darker areas while brightening and losing detail in lighter areas. This filter works in a similar way to Film Grain (see page 18) in that a random pattern is applied to the image shadow areas, and is controlled primarily by the Highlight Area and Intensity sliders.

How it works

1 With all sliders centralized (5, 10, and 5) the result is a reasonable approximation of a sketch made with broad soft pastels (but probably not a stick).

2 Settings of 10, 10, and 2 produce an interesting sculptural effect, where the stroke pattern extends out from the shadow areas.

3 Slightly varied settings (10, 20, 5) can work equally well on a monochrome subject.

4 The same settings (10, 20, 5) applied to the target image clearly show the diagonal displacement that drives this filter.

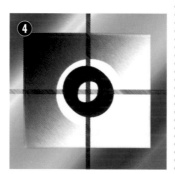

Using the Smudge Stick filter

Smudge Stick is another filter that needs immediate work after application. Its basic effect is reminiscent of watercolor, but it gives more interesting results when used with other filters.

1 The African cheetah makes a suitable target, already blessed with one natural application of Smudge Stick.

2 Duplicate the existing layer and apply the Smudge Stick filter at Stroke Length 10, Highlight Area 8, and Intensity 8. Apart from the obvious smudging, the initial application has unearthed some previously unseen detail in the background and raised the contrast level.

3a–c Try changing the blending mode and reducing the opacity. The Pin Light mode adds warmth overall.

4 Copy the filtered layer (Ctrl/Cmd+A, Ctrl/Cmd+C), click on the Channels tab, and then on the New Channel icon.

5 Paste the copied image into the new alpha channel. It will appear as grayscale in the palette.

6 Apply the Bas Relief filter (from the Sketch menu—see page 130) set to Detail 15, Smoothness 8, with a Top Left lighting direction.

7 Click on the RGB thumbnail in the Channels palette to make it visible, then return to the Layers palette. You can now use the new alpha channel as a texture map using Lighting Effects from the Render menu (see page 118).

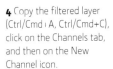

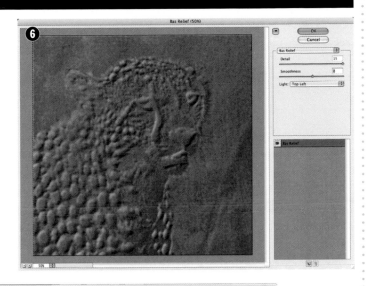

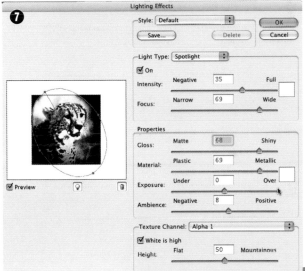

Underpainting

This filter is laid out in the same way as Rough Pastels (see page 32), but gives a very different result. Real underpainting generally uses an abbreviated palette compared with the finished work, and often employs patches of contrasting color that are designed to subtly affect the top coat of pigment. See the Filter Gallery feature on page 6 to see how Underpainting can easily be used in combination with other filters.

How it works

1 At its most basic, it's perfect for that once-in-a-lifetime need to simulate a mural on a brick wall. Choose Brush Size 0, Texture Coverage 10, Texture Brick, Scaling 200%, and Relief 10.

2 Here is the target image treated with Burlap. You can see where the filter has worked on the edges in the image, but not the flat color.

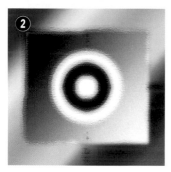

Using the Underpainting filter

Since Underpainting only works along image edges, it's necessary to recruit another effect to get a decent result.

1 A strong simple shape is ideal for this concerted attack.

2 Duplicate the existing layer twice by dragging it onto the Create new layer (turned page) icon at the foot of the Layers palette.

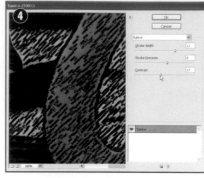

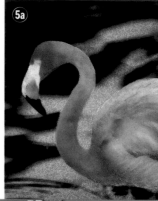

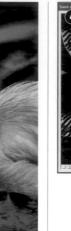

5a, 5b Change the blending mode to Linear Light.

6 Move to the top layer and change the blending mode to Pin Light.

7 The translucent blending modes of the top two layers allow the background to show through, contributing to the overall effect.

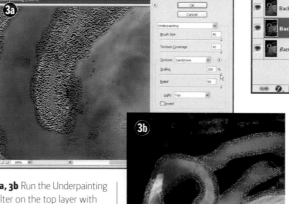

3a, 3b Run the Underpainting filter on the top layer with all sliders at maximum, Texture set to Sandstone, and Light set to Top Left.

4 Turn off the upper, filtered layer and apply the Sumi-e filter (under **Filter > Brush Strokes**—see page 71) to the middle layer in the stack. Set Stroke Width 11, Stroke Pressure 8, and Contrast 17.

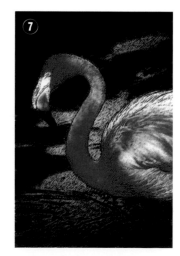

Watercolor

Watercolor has long been a defining Photoshop filter, though the crucial illusion of one color running into its neighbor is only partly achieved. Use the Smudge or Healing Brush tool to help the illusion. If you're looking to imitate gouache painting, however, search no further—the slight darkening around the edge of each patch of color perfectly reproduces the effect of this more opaque pigment.

How it works

1 The dialog box offers three sliders. Though Brush Detail can be invoked across the whole scale, the remaining controls usually make a color image impossibly dark once pushed past the halfway mark.

2 Settings of 14, 14, and 1 will produce a reasonably painterly result.

3 On a monochrome image a "stippled" appearance results from setting Brush Detail at 14, and both Shadow Intensity and Texture at 3.

Although it's tempting to be gentle with this filter, often what's required is bravura painting.

1 The ocean scene and distant prospects provide scope for brushwork.

2 Apply the filter to test the waters. Here, we've used Brush Detail 14, Shadow Intensity 1, Texture 1. As you can see, the initial application is excessively dark.

3 It's a good moment to retreat and try another approach. Go back to the original, and this time use **Blur > Motion Blur** with a Distance of 6 pixels to break up the image details.

4 Continue with the Diffuse filter from the Stylize menu. Choose Lighten Only and apply the filter several times in succession by selecting **Filter > Diffuse** (or Ctrl/ Cmd+F).

5 Finally, apply the Watercolor filter again but with Brush Detail 14, Shadow Intensity 0, and Texture 3. The result is not a bad approximation of a watercolor painting.

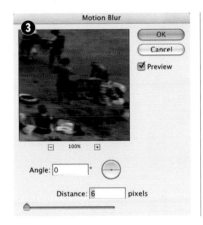

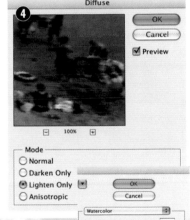

37

The Blur filters

Why bother to blur? A digital photographer with a large investment in quality lenses and a camera or two with high resolution capabilities might wonder about the virtues of Photoshop's Blur filter suite. In fact, it contains effects that are almost as useful as those in the Sharpen collection. The Average filter, for example, introduced in Photoshop CS, can help beef up thin originals, and Lens Blur, another innovation, can produce convincing optical blur effects quite unlike those offered by Blur and Gaussian Blur. Smart Blur can subtly improve pictures taken under difficult conditions—smoothing out noise artefacts at the pixel level. Innovations in CS2 are Box Blur, Shape Blur, and Surface Blur. In many cases, blur of one kind or another can help redeem images that have been over-sharpened in previous attempts at enhancement.

page 39—Average

page 40—Blur

page 41—Box Blur

page 42—Gaussian Blur

page 45—Lens Blur

page 50—Radial Blur

page 52—Shape Blur

page 54—Smart Blur

38

Average

Average calculates the amount of each color in the original image and produces a one-color visual soup with the result. No controls are offered, since none are needed. To get rid of irritating noise patterns (or tone down over-energetic applications of the Noise filter) use Average.

How it works

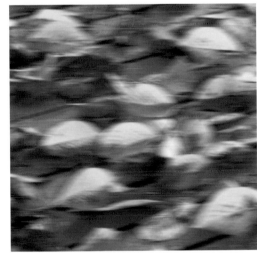

1 An image of fall leaves unsurprisingly gives a mid-brown result.

2 Applying it to the multicolored target produces a mid-gray, since almost all colors are equally present in the original image.

1 This vestigial shot of smoke against a dead black background looks beyond rescue. Lighting was kept to the minimum to avoid illuminating the background and losing the smoke.

2 An application of the Curves adjustment on the Auto setting reveals a great deal of valuable detail, and a large amount of noise.

3 Duplicate this layer, and run the Average filter on it. The result is a murky gray.

4 To reveal the smoke layer beneath, we now need to change the blending mode of this layer to Soft Light.

5 Though there are still signs of noise in the smoke trails, on balance this is a better picture than the original.

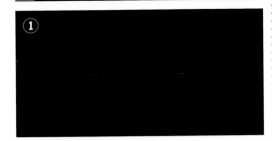

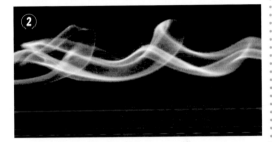

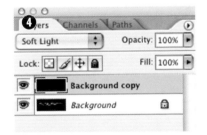

page 40—Blur More

page 48—Motion Blur

page 56—Surface Blur

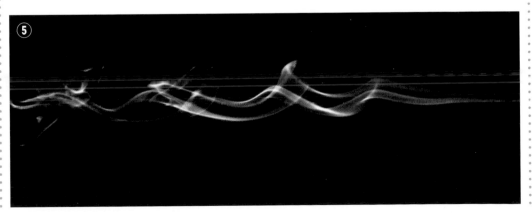

Blur and Blur More

Blur works by averaging pixel colors wherever it discovers distinct edges in the image—alongside shadow areas, for example. With no controls over the extent of the pixels to be averaged, it's useful only as a quick fix when you're in a great hurry.

How it works

1 One application of the filter has a slight effect, which is not easily perceived at this size.

2a–c Repeating the effect once (2a), twice (2b), and three times (2c) shows the cumulative effect at the pixel level.

3 A fourth application appears to have greatly blurred the image in close-up.

4 However, at normal size the effect is only just noticeable.

Blur More

The one-shot stablemate to Blur, Blur More has a stronger effect—three to four times that of regular Blur. The lack of control, though, means that this filter is still of little real use.

How it works

5 The effect of a single application of Blur More is not easily perceived at this size.

6 At the pixel level you can see the stronger effect...

7 ...compared with one application of regular Blur.

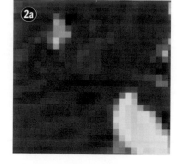
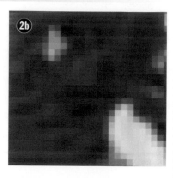

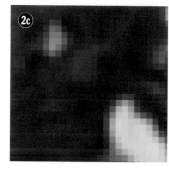

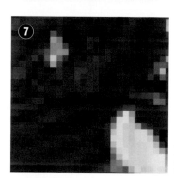
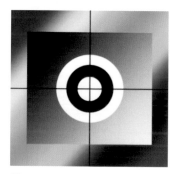

Using the Blur and Blur More filters

It's difficult and very unrewarding to attempt to differentiate Blur from Blur More. The best strategy is not to use these ineffectual filters—blur is a delicate instrument and needs to be finely controlled.

Blur

Blur More

Box Blur

Newly introduced in Photoshop CS2, Box Blur operates by changing the color of pixels based on the color of other pixels nearby. Think of it as a quicker and dirtier version of Gaussian Blur (see page 42). The panel offers only a single slider to define the radius of action.

How it works

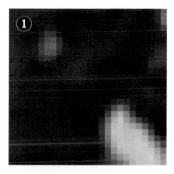

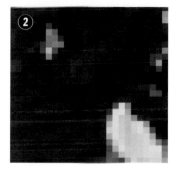

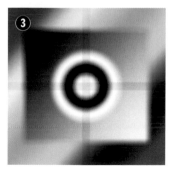

1 The result at one pixel radius is shown magnified.

2 Compare it with the untreated version to see the difference that just a single pixel radius blur can have.

3 The target image quickly breaks into the characteristic box pattern with applications at a 10-pixel radius.

Freed from the constraints of conventional photographic blur, you can use Box Blur, for example, to create optically illogical blur.

1, 2 This bleak original has a strong asymmetrical axis which suggests the obvious area to define with the Lasso tool.

3 Feather the resulting selection. As a guide, set the Feather Radius to about a tenth of the pixel width of the full image.

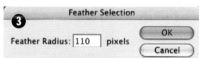

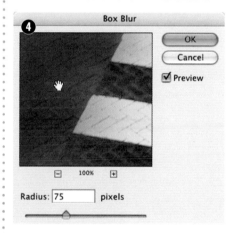

4 Invert the selection (Ctrl/Cmd+Shift+I) and go to **Filter > Blur > Box Blur** and set the Radius to 75. You may need to use the Hand tool (click and drag in the Preview window) to see the blurred area.

5 The result shows the characteristic rectangular pattern of Box Blur.

6 With the selection still active, use **Image > Adjustments > Auto Color** (or Ctrl/Cmd+Shift+B) to restore some strength to the blurred area.

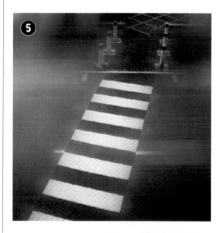

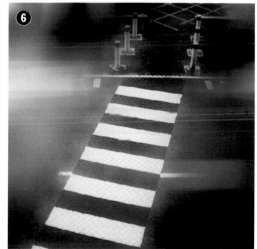

Gaussian Blur

Where Blur and Blur More operate by adding averaged pixels along defined edges, Gaussian Blur looks beyond these edges to include more distant pixels. This "search radius" is controlled by the slider in the dialog box.

How it works

1a, 1b Even at as low a setting as 1.2 pixels, the effect is noticeable.

2 At a setting of 15 pixels radius the image is practically unrecognizable.

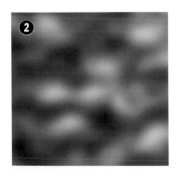

Using the Gaussian Blur filter

Use selective Gaussian blur to add emphasis and structure to pictures.

1 This image could use some treatment to enhance the atmosphere of isolation.

2 Choose the Elliptical Marquee tool and set Feather to 200 pixels (this image is 1400 pixels wide).

Feather: 200 px

3 Click and drag the marquee to enclose the center of interest. Select Inverse (Ctrl/Cmd+Shift+I).

4 Apply Gaussian Blur to a Radius value of 9.

5a, 5b With the selection still active, the defocused area can be treated further with Hue/Saturation, for example, with the Colorize button checked.

6 Here, the Saturation has been reduced almost to monochrome and the Lightness level raised. Changing the Hue value introduces a slight purple cast to the selection.

Hue/Saturation

Master

Hue: 245

Saturation: 10

Lightness: +10

OK
Cancel
Load...
Save...

☑ Colorize
☑ Preview

Gaussian Blur

OK
Cancel
☑ Preview

17%

Radius: 9 pixels

Lens Blur

Photographers will find themselves right at home with Lens Blur. With this filter, Photoshop has firmly resolved to speak the photographic language. In fact, there are more controls here than are found on many professional cameras and lenses.

How it works

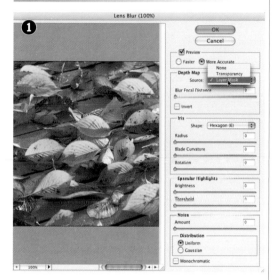

1 The critical item in the Lens Blur dialog box is the Depth Map. On this page we'll show just a couple of simple examples of how it controls the effect of the filter. On page 46 you'll find a more detailed investigation. The Depth Map can be based on the image's own areas of transparency, or, more usefully, on a Layer Mask alpha channel that you create to define foreground and background areas (assuming a conventional photograph where nearer areas are at the foot of the image). The black areas of the mask denote parts of the image nearest the camera, while white areas are at the back. You can easily reverse this setup by checking the Invert box. Alternatively, select None as the Layer Mask for a more straightforward blur effect that's controlled by the Iris dialog. The Blur Focal Distance slider runs from 1 (near to the camera) to 255 (far from the camera).

2 To check out the Alpha channel function, open your image and make sure that Channels is checked in the Window menu. In the Channels tab, click on the button at top right and select New Channel.

3 Hit OK in the dialog box and you'll see the new channel appear, named by default Alpha 1.

4, 5 Select the Gradient tool from the Toolbox (make sure that black is selected as the foreground color and white as the background), click the Gradient picker in the Toolbar at the top of the screen, and choose the Foreground to Background preset gradient.

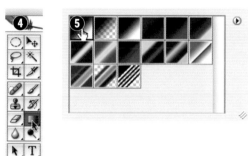

6 Finally, ensure that you have Linear Gradient selected as the type.

7 Use the gradient tool to draw a straight line from the bottom to the top of the Alpha Channel window—hold down Shift if necessary to keep the gradient straight. You'll see the gradient appear at the foot of the Channels tab.

8 Click on the RGB channel (or CMYK if appropriate) and return to the Layers palette. Select **Filter > Blur > Lens Blur**. Choose Alpha 1 as the Source of the Depth Map, and set Blur Focal Distance to zero. Set the Iris controls to around quarter-strength, and all of the remaining controls to zero.

9 With these settings, the image foreground is sharp, with the blur effect increasing as it moves toward the background.

How it works continued

10 Setting the Blur Focal Distance slider to halfway moves the sharp area to midway in the image.

11 With the slider at its full extent (255) the sharp area shifts to the background.

12 For the record, the target image (at the same settings as 10) clearly shows how Lens Blur differs from regular Blur. The vertical line becomes increasingly blurred as it moves out from the centerof the image.

13 The Iris function works in conjunction with the Specular Highlights feature—with no specular highlights, Iris has no effect. The real photographic iris, or diaphragm, is made from a number of thin overlapping blades secured to a rotating ring. As the ring turns, the light-admitting aperture is enlarged or reduced. When the subject includes bright points of light, their out-of-focus image reflects the number of blades in the mechanism. Photoshop CS has enthusiastically reproduced this phenomenon with six iris types and three sliders.

14 At these settings, the six-sided highlights are just about detectable in this greatly enlarged section of the background of the fall leaves image.

15 The Radius slider acts in imitation of the real photographic aperture, though with the numerical values reversed. At zero (which is, let's say, the equivalent of f32 on a real lens) the whole image is sharp, while at 100 (f2.8, or full aperture) only a narrow band remains in focus. Blade

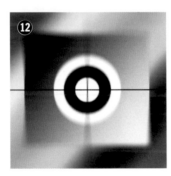

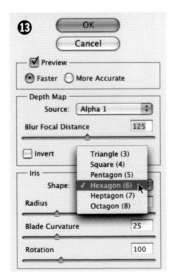

Curvature makes the highlights less or more round, while Rotation enables you to turn the axis of the highlights. In the Specular Highlights dialog, Brightness controls the strength of highlights, while Threshold determines the level at which light areas qualify as highlights. These controls need to be carefully adjusted on the merits of each image. With both set to maximum, an ugly mess is produced.

16 The Noise dialog offers the same facilities as the **Filter > Noise > Add Noise** effect, and needs to be used equally sparingly.

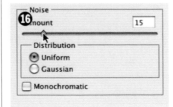

You can extend the normal envelope of photographic blur by using the facilities within the Lens Blur filter together with special selection techniques.

1 The original image was shot at extreme wide-angle (inherently giving large depth-of-field) with strong backlighting ("contre-jour").

2 Make a selection of the part to keep sharp using the Elliptical marquee tool.

3 Now to rotate the marquee, but not the selection within it. Right-click/Ctrl+click to bring up a secondary dialog. Choose Transform Selection.

4 Use the regular handles to rotate the selection off-axis.

5 Click the check mark in the Options bar when the rotated selection is in the right place.

6 With the rotated selection still active, open the Channels palette and create a new channel by clicking on the turned-page icon.

7 Go to Select > Feather and choose a 50 pixel radius.

Deselect
Select Inverse
Feather...

Save Selection...
Make Work Path...

Layer via Copy
Layer via Cut
Layer...

Free Transform
Transform Selection

Fill...
Stroke...

Lens Blur
Fade...

6

	RGB	⌘~
	Red	⌘1
	Green	⌘2
	Blue	⌘3
👁	Alpha 1	⌘4

Feather Selection

7

Feather Radius: 50 pixels

OK Cancel

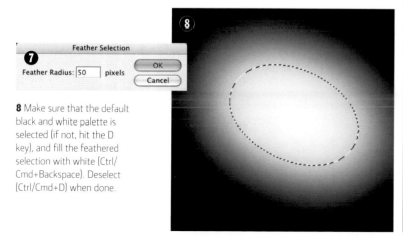

8 Make sure that the default black and white palette is selected (if not, hit the D key), and fill the feathered selection with white (Ctrl/Cmd+Backspace). Deselect (Ctrl/Cmd+D) when done.

9, 10 Return to the Channels palette and click the RGB thumbnail. Use **Blur > Lens Blur** to control the area of sharp focus. Select the Alpha channel as the Depth map, and check Invert.

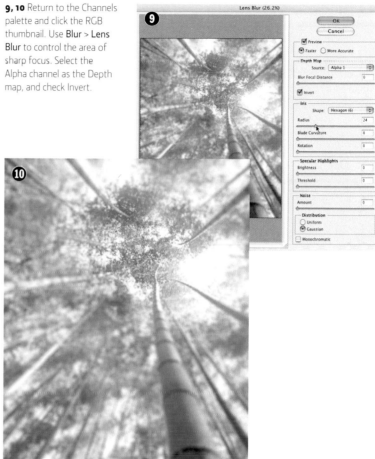

11 An alternative and lighter effect can be obtained by adding small values via the Brightness and Threshold sliders in the Specular Highlights area of the panel.

45

Motion Blur

Motion Blur is of limited use on its own. The dialog box offers just direction and distance, and the results are very much as you'd expect them to be. See the following example for uses of the Motion Blur filter in combination with other effects.

How it works

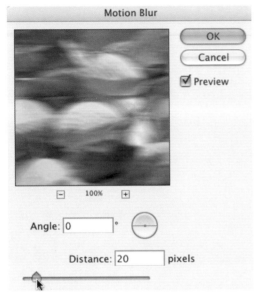

1 At settings of Angle 0°, Distance 20, the result could be pressed into service as a background or wallpaper.

2 Try changing the Angle to 45° and pushing the Distance slider to halfway for a heavily blurred wash of color.

3 Finally, try pushing the filter as far as it will go: 90° and maximum Distance (999 pixels) for a fall colors candy-stripe result.

4 Using the target image, a curious effect is obtained by setting Angle 0° and Distance 100 pixels.

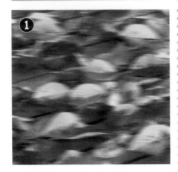

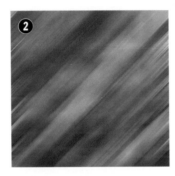

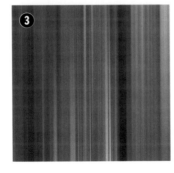

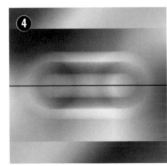

Using the Motion Blur filter

To get localized "speed lines" use the Layer via Copy feature in conjunction with the Motion Blur filter.

1 Select the Lasso tool and set its Feather value to 100 pixels in the Tool Options bar (the main image is 1500 pixels wide).

2 Alt/Option-click to make a selection around one vehicle. Alternatively, just draw the shape freehand by dragging.

3 With the feathered selection active, go to **Layer > New > Layer via Copy** (Ctrl/Cmd+J).

4 The selected area forms a new active layer and the selection marquee disappears.

5 Use Motion Blur at the maximum value. Ensure the Angle setting follows the direction of travel. Click OK.

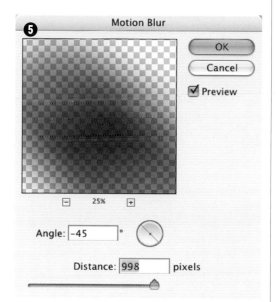

Motion Blur

OK
Cancel
☑ Preview

─ 25% ＋

Angle: -45 °

Distance: 998 pixels

6 Select the Eraser tool, and choose a soft brush from the Brush Presets Picker in the Tool Options bar. If you have a pressure-sensitive stylus and tablet set-up, click on the Airbrush icon in the same menu to make use of the variable stroke-width facilities—you can also reduce the Opacity and Flow settings.

7 Carefully erase the motion blur effect from the vehicle. You can, however, choose to retain some streaks on the vehicle sides wherever they help the illusion.

8, 9 Turn off visibility of the underlying layer from time to time to check the progress of erasing.

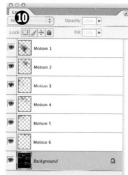
Eraser Diameter 45 px

Hardness: 0%

17
21
27
35
45
65
100

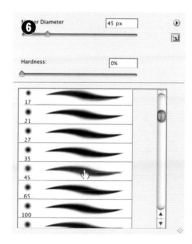

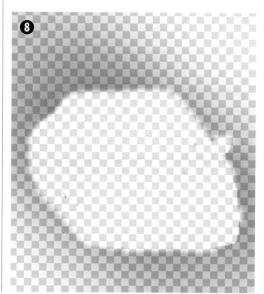

10 If you're patient enough, each vehicle can be treated in the same way.

11 In this case, all the Layer blending modes have been left at Normal, but it's worth experimenting with other settings like Lighten and Screen for similar images.

47

Radial Blur

This effect, like Motion Blur, dates from Photoshop's earliest days. The alternative Quality levels in the dialog box speak of underpowered machines struggling for hours to render filter effects.

How it works

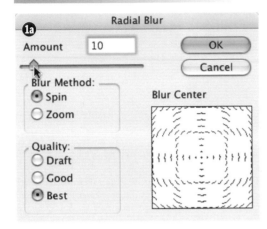

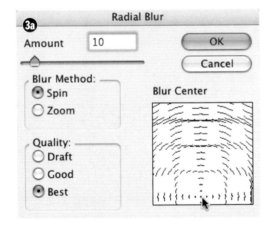

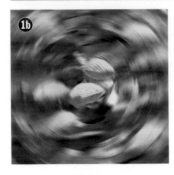

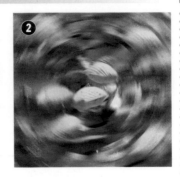

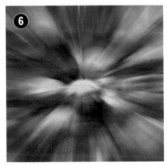

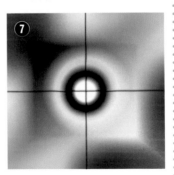

1a, 1b Setting the Amount to 10, the Method to Spin, and the Quality to Best gives this wormhole effect.

2 If you perversely choose Draft at the same settings, you'll be rewarded with a strangely painterly result.

3a, 3b One further control is available in the Blur Center window. You can click and drag in this window to re-center the Spin effect.

4 The Zoom function shares the same controls. At Amount 10, there is a light streaking radiating from the image center.

5 Increasing the setting to 40 strengthens the zoom lens effect.

6 Using the maximum zoom amount breaks up the image completely.

7 The target image, incidentally, produces an interesting effect at maximum setting.

Using the Radial Blur filter

Although you can alter the Blur Center in the Radial Blur dialog box, it can be difficult to judge exactly where the center will end up on your image—especially if your image is not square. In these cases, it's often easier to leave the dialog box at its default position and move the image itself to accurately place the blur.

1 The intended center of this blur is shown by the red cross scrawled on a new layer—add some guides as well if you like.

2a, 2b Use Photoshop's rulers or the Measure tool to find out how much needs to be added to the short sides to move the cross to the middle. Use **Image** > **Canvas Size** to add the space, and click in the top right corner of the Anchor box to ensure the additional space arrives in the right place. Hit OK.

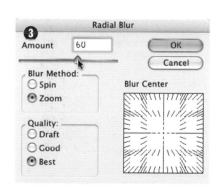

Canvas Size

Current Size: 8.10M
Width: 1888 pixels
Height: 1499 pixels

OK
Cancel

New Size: 12.6M
Width: 2200 pixels
Height: 2000 pixels

☐ Relative
Anchor:

Canvas extension color: Background

3 Make sure the original image layer is active, choose Zoom and Best Quality in the Radial Blur filter. Hit OK.

Radial Blur

Amount 60

OK
Cancel

Blur Method:
○ Spin
◉ Zoom

Blur Center

Quality:
○ Draft
○ Good
◉ Best

25%   Doc: 12.6M/11.3M

4 The effect is centered on the required area.

5 Use the Crop tool to remove the surplus canvas.

The image will necessarily be slightly smaller than the original because of the encroachment of the filter effect in the lower left corner.

49

Shape Blur

Shape Blur is new in Photoshop CS2 and uses the application's existing Shapes presets as the basis for a special non-optical blur. The shape provides the basis for the filter kernel. Some of the more complex presets—envelopes and thumbtacks, for example—are obviously not candidates, but the simpler graphic shapes can produce interesting results. You can also import the entire Shape library and experiment further.

How it works

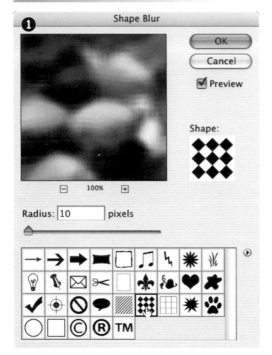

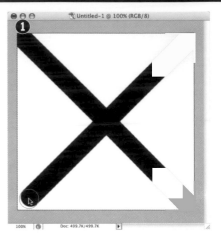

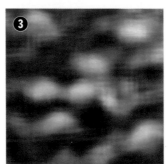

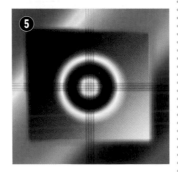

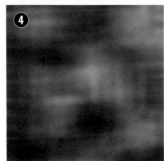

1, 2 The filter opens with a single slider and a view of the Shapes presets. Choosing the diagonal checkers shape at the minimum setting gives a lightly blurred effect with a strong residual pattern from the chosen shape.

3 Increasing the pixel radius first to 20...

4 ...and then 50 increases the blur while reducing the strength of the underlying shape. Be careful when increasing the pixel radius to a large amount, as it quickly becomes demanding on your computer's processor.

5 Here's the target image subjected to the "Grid" shape at a 10 pixel radius.

Using the Shape Blur filter

There's a great variety of preset Shapes in the Shape Blur menu (304 in total if you choose Append All in the fly-out menu) but the majority are of no use with this filter. Try making your own custom shape as the kernel for Shape Blur.

1 Make a new document. This one is around 400 pixels square but, since the end of the process is a vector shape, resolution is not dependent on the starting image size. Take a fat brush with maximum hardness, and draw corner to corner while holding down the Shift key.

2 Plant the Magic Wand tool in the black area and click to select the cross shape.

3 Move to the Paths tab and select Make Work Path from the fly-out menu.

4 When the Make Work Path dialog appears, choose the tightest tolerance (0.5 pixels) and hit OK.

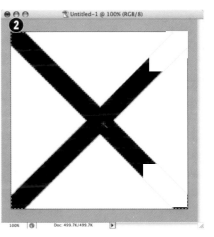

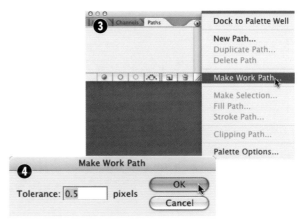

50

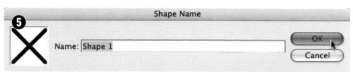

5 Go to the Edit menu and select Define Custom Shape. In the resulting Shape Name dialog you can name your new shape, but it's not really necessary. Neither is there any need to save this document, now that the shape has been defined.

6 Open the document to be treated and use the Elliptical Marquee tool to outline the face. Go to **Select > Feather** to soften the selection. The original is 1600 pixels wide—the feather radius chosen is 30 pixels. Invert the selection (Ctrl/Cmd+Shift+I), and hide it (Ctrl/Cmd+H) to make the subsequent filter action easier to see.

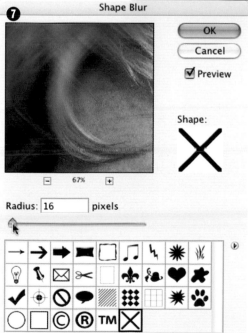

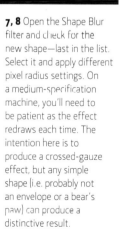

7, 8 Open the Shape Blur filter and check for the new shape—last in the list. Select it and apply different pixel radius settings. On a medium-specification machine, you'll need to be patient as the effect redraws each time. The intention here is to produce a crossed-gauze effect, but any simple shape (i.e. probably not an envelope or a bear's paw) can produce a distinctive result.

Smart Blur

Though similar in function to Gaussian Blur, Smart Blur adds some useful features, making it more precise. The filter might equally well have been called Clean Up, and housed under the Sharpen menu.

How it works

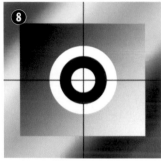

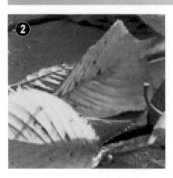

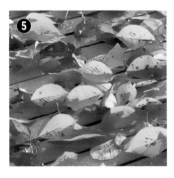

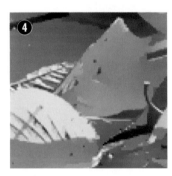

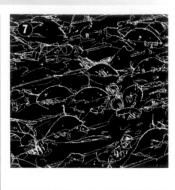

1 The dialog box offers Radius and Threshold controls, settings for Low, Medium, and High quality, and three Modes: Normal, Edge Only, and Overlay Edge.

2 Compare the greatly magnified but untreated original image...

3 ...with this version that has been treated with the filter at settings: Radius 20, Threshold 20, Quality High, Mode Normal. Though the result may look extreme at this scale, the effect is only just perceptible at normal size, and is very effective in clearing up the noise that often occurs in digital photographs.

4, 5 Setting both sliders at a more extreme level (80) begins to flatten the image into colored patches.

6a, 6b Also apparently lodged in the wrong category are the accompanying Edge Only (6a) and Overlay Edge (6b) effects. These search for color transitions only—the first applies white to the edges and obscures the rest of the original image with black, while the second applies white edges only, letting the original image show through.

7 Careful manipulation of the sliders with the Edge Only function selected results in a detailed map of adjacent color edge changes. This can be blurred conventionally and used as a mask in an alpha channel (see the following example) or to form the basis for other graphic effects.

8 With few boundaries for it to work on, the Smart Blur filter has very little effect on the target image.

52

Using the Smart Blur filter

You can use Smart Blur's edge detection facilities to create special effects which have nothing to do with blur.

1 The image is already full of texture and strong edge contrast. The first step is to duplicate the image.

2 Select **Filter > Blur > Smart Blur** and set Mode to Edge Only. Set Radius 7, and Threshold 30. Unless you're blessed with a fast machine, start off by exploiting Smart Blur in Low Quality.

3 To add some extra grit to the original image, simply change the Layer blending mode of the "Low" filtered version to Multiply and reduce its Opacity to 60%.

4 To use the filtered image as an Alpha Channel, first restore its Opacity to 100%, then select all (Ctrl/Cmd+A), copy (Ctrl/Cmd+C) and open the Channels palette. Click on the New Channel icon.

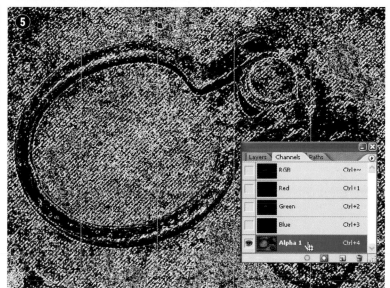

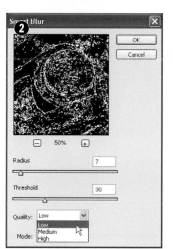

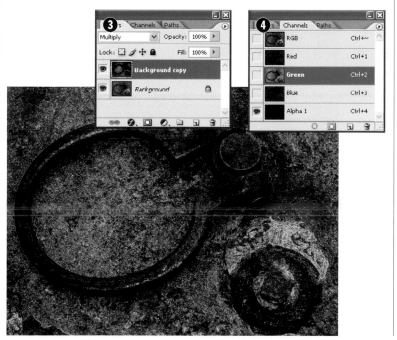

5 Paste (Ctrl/Cmd+V) the image into the new channel, then Ctrl/Cmd+click its thumbnail to activate the selection. You'll see the characteristic "marching ants" on screen.

6a–e Click on the RGB thumbnail, return to the main Layers palette and activate the original untreated image (hide the other layer and hide the selection as well by keying Ctrl/Cmd+H, so that you can see filtration effects more easily). Almost any one of the more aggressive Artistic, Brush Strokes, or Sketch filters can now be used at around half-strength to affect this restricted selection. In this example, from left to right are: (6a) the untreated image; (6b) Poster Edges; (6c) Watercolor; (6d) Crosshatch; (6e) Graphic Pen.

53

Surface Blur

The final component in the Blur suite is Surface Blur, another innovation in CS2. The "surface" in question is any area not exhibiting edge characteristics. Blurring is confined to flat, slowly gradating, or normally textured parts of the picture, while edges remain distinct. The effect is unlike the conventional "optical" blurs at almost every setting.

How it works

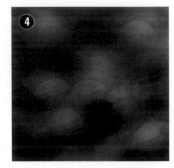

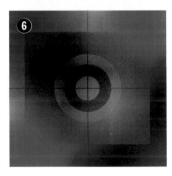

1 Surface Blur offers the traditional pair of sliders. Radius determines how far the net should be spread when looking for likely pixels, and Threshold controls the amount of blurring. At these low values the effect is very slight.

2 Raising the radius to 20 pixels begins to flatten out the non-edge areas.

3 At 40-pixel settings on both sliders, there is considerable blurring of non-edge areas, while edges are still distinct.

4 Leaving the Radius setting at 40 and advancing the Threshold to 200, you'll see a vestigial image highly reminiscent of very early photography, in which the only resolved areas are those with high-contrast edges.

5 Cranking both sliders to maximum still leaves a detectable image.

6 At the same settings, the target image also retains its linear structure and contrast edges amid a mist of color.

Using the Surface Blur filter

This filter has obvious practical uses in noise suppression, but possesses other qualities worth exploiting as well. Here, its effect on detail edges is used as the basis for a filigree "drawn" effect which is subsequently overlaid and blended with the original photograph.

1, 2 Open a copy of the original, duplicate the layer (Ctrl/Cmd+J) and treat it with Surface Blur.

3 Invert the filtered layer (Ctrl/Cmd+I) and change its blending mode to Color Dodge.

4 The barely perceptible result shows only the detail edges found by Surface Blur.

5, 6 To retrieve the image, merge the layers and go to **Image > Adjustments > Levels**. Compress the Input Levels slider to the right and increase the Output Levels shadow value. Hit OK.

7, 8 Copy this filtered layer, paste it back on to the original photograph, and change its blending mode to Multiply. The effect has picked out a lot of extra "drawn" detail in the image, while still retaining some photographic qualities.

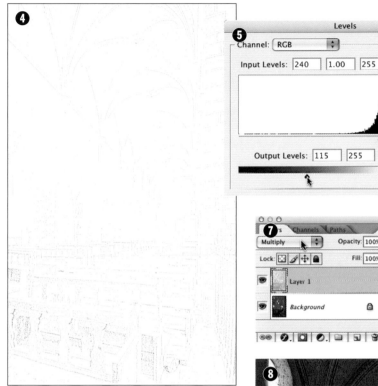

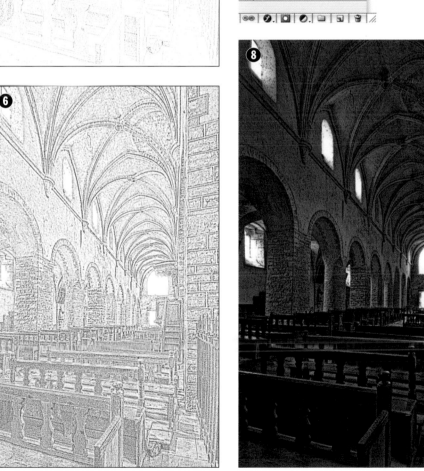

The Brush Stroke filters

Much effort has been expended on refining the Brush tool throughout the development of Photoshop, culminating in the comprehensive Brush palette of the latest versions, which is equipped with a vast array of brush tips and behaviors. The Brush Strokes filter suite, however, has ancient origins and, apart from interface changes, has rumbled along almost unchanged through many upgrades. The logic of this collection is that it is strictly limited to the tool used for painting—for surfaces, canvases, substrates, and brick walls you have to go to the Sketch menu. And despite the only approximate resemblance of any given filter effect to its real-world namesake, there are some effective techniques to be gleaned here. For the photographer seeking alternatives to the straight digital approach, a Brush Strokes filter allied with the Edit > Fade command can provide an interesting diversion.

The Brush Stroke filters

page 59—Dark Strokes

page 60—Accented Edges

page 62—Angled Strokes

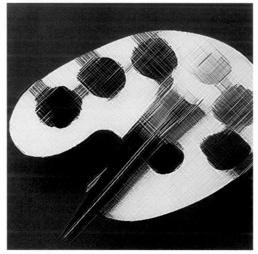
page 64—Crosshatch

page 66—Ink Outlines

page 69—Spatter

page 70—Sprayed Strokes

page 71—Sumi-e

56

Dark Strokes

This filter paints over an image in a mix of dark and light strokes. Balance controls the extent to which the effect overcomes the image, while the two Intensity sliders operate black strokes in dark areas and white strokes in lighter parts. Try the Dark Strokes filter for adding contrast to images, and introducing a lacquered, shiny appearance.

How it works

1 Keep the Black Intensity level low to avoid overwhelming the original image. Here, the settings are Balance 3, Black Intensity 1, White Intensity 10.

Using the Dark Strokes filter

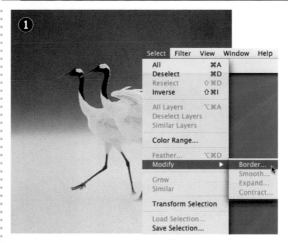

A humble use for the Dark Strokes filter that also exploits a small Photoshop aberration. The intention is to create a simple informal border within the existing image.

1 Select all (Ctrl/Cmd+A) and go to Select > Modify. The only option available is Border, which will produce a soft selection with a maximum size of 200 pixels. If you want a regular hard-edged smaller selection, you'll have to draw it by eye, or use Guides.

2 The marquee appears—this image is 1700 pixels wide, and this selection is insufficiently large.

3 Now if you go to Select > Modify again, you can click on the Expand option. The resulting dialog will allow a figure of up to 100 pixels.

4 Go to **Filter > Brush Strokes > Dark Strokes** and in the bottom left-hand corner of the filter window select Fit on Screen so that the entire image becomes visible. Set values Balance 2, Black Integrity 2, and White Integrity 6. Click OK.

5 Deselect the selection. The image has a noticeably darker border.

57

Accented Edges

The Accented Edges filter lives up to its name by drawing black or white outlines around significant edges in your images.

How it works

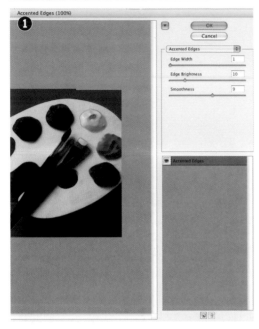

1 Three sliders control Edge Width, Edge Brightness, and Smoothness. Edge Width runs from 1 to 14 pixels, and the outline starts off black irrespective of the color setting in the Toolbox. Edge Brightness gradually suffuses the outline with white, and invades the surrounding areas at maximum strength while Smoothness imparts a progressive blur.

2 With Edge Brightness at a low value, Edge Width also has to be kept low to get a reasonably bright result such as this, where the settings were 2, 20, and 10 respectively.

3 Increasing Edge Brightness by 10 has a very positive effect, and the close-up view shows the erosion of the image edges.

4 When Smoothness is reduced to minimum, the image reverts to a more photographic appearance with aggressive highlights.

5 A quasi-neon effect can be achieved by pushing all of the sliders to the limit.

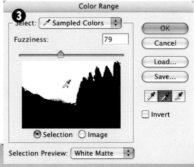

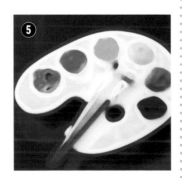

Using the Accented Edges filter

If you're still looking for a better watercolor filter than the Watercolor filter, some hope is at hand with Accented Edges.

1, 2 First, there's an opportunity to rescue the featureless sky in this image. Click in a typical sky area with the Eyedropper tool.

3 Go to **Select > Color Range**. You'll find that some of the sky is already selected. Click on the center Eyedropper icon—the one with a plus sign—and click in other areas of the sky to gradually select all shades of blue. It's sometimes easier to use the Eyedropper on the full-color image itself, for the same result. In either case, click OK when the preview looks complete.

4 The selected area is shown by the "marching ants."

5 Color Range selections often need correction, as here, where the blue component of the distant hill has been included in the main selection. Just take the Lasso tool, hold down the Alt/Option key and carve away the surplus selection.

6 Choose the Gradient tool from the toolbox and ensure that Linear Gradient (the first option in the menu bar) is selected. The Toolbox palette should show blue in the foreground from the Eyedropper exercise at step 2, and the background should be white, as the default. Starting near the top of the sky, draw downward through the sky area with the Gradient tool. Hold down the Shift key to keep the line vertical.

7, 8, 9 Apply the Mezzotint filter (from the Pixelate menu—see page 108), selecting Medium Strokes from the pull-down menu, and immediately fade it with **Edit > Fade Mezzotint,** using Pin Light at 50%.

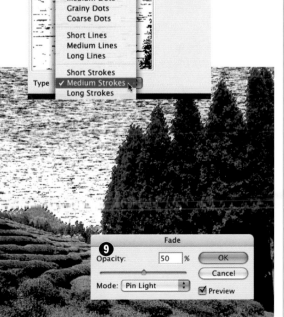

10 With the selection still active, use the Gaussian Blur filter set to a Radius of around 4 pixels to soften the sky effect. Deselect.

11, 12 Now, finally, apply Accented Edges with Edge Width 7, Edge Brightness 20, and Smoothness 15, for a dark watercolor result.

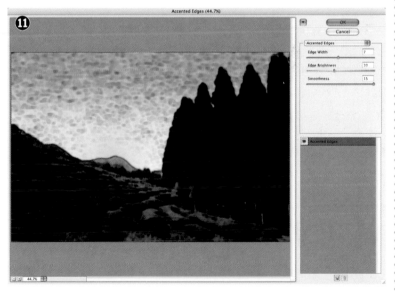

Angled Strokes

Use the Angled Strokes filter to introduce an edgy, geometric quality to flat originals. This filter behaves more like a sharp-edged version of Motion Blur than an actual brushstroke. The most significant slider in the control panel is Direction Balance. Low values (0-50) favor the top-left to bottom-right axis for stroking; higher values give more emphasis in the diagonally opposite direction.

How it works

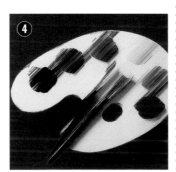

1 Closer examination of this image processed with Direction Balance 28, Stroke Length 25, and Sharpness 5 shows the effect in detail. Look at the blob of green paint—the red trails are not its complementary color, but have been introduced from the background.

2 Changing the background color to blue and re-running the filter with the same settings proves the point. The bottom-left to top-right axis is curiously less powerful than its companion.

3 With the Direction Balance slider set to 90—nearly at its limit—and all of the other settings untouched, the effect is muted.

4 Raising the Stroke Length control to nearly its maximum reveals its effect on the filter.

Using the Angled Strokes filter

One of the more aggressive Brush Strokes filters, and strictly mechanical in appearance, Angled Strokes needs to be diluted.

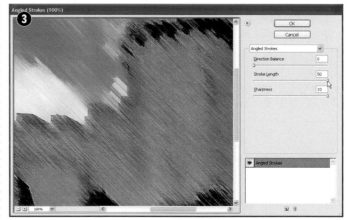

1, 2 Start by duplicating the original image twice in the Layers palette.

3, 4 Open **Filter > Brush Strokes > Angled Strokes** and apply it to the top layer with values of Direction Balance 0, Stroke Length 50, and Sharpness 10.

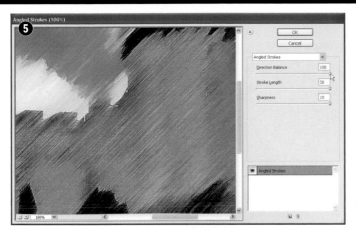

9 You can continue to experiment on these two layers with many different blending modes. What's really required is a systematic approach, and one possibility is to use the Layer Group feature in Photoshop. Click on the folder icon at the foot of the Layers palette.

10 Click and drag the topmost layer thumbnail into the Group 1 layer. Do the same with the second filtered layer. The locked Background layer, however, will refuse to be moved. In any case, for this exercise it's best to leave it in place.

11 Click on the Group 1 icon to open the group and reveal the enclosed layers. If you need to move a layer out of a group, just drag its thumbnail leftward until it jumps back into the normal alignment. Notice that the Layer Group has gained its own blending mode, set to Pass Through as the default. This means that the blending modes within the group will act in the same away as if they were

outside it. You can easily duplicate the Layer Group by dragging its thumbnail on to the New Layer icon. Do so now to create a copy of our current group.

12, 13 Click on the Group 1 eyeball icon to hide it. Now you can change the blending mode (and the opacity) of the layers contained within the duplicated group. Here, the lower layer is at 60% opacity with the blending mode changed to Hard Mix. The upper layer is at 50% opacity, set to Linear Burn. This way, you can easily save layer groups that are successful, duplicate them at will for further modification, and drag the failures to the Trash icon at the foot of the palette.

5, 6 Hide the top layer in the Layers palette (click the eye icon) and make the next layer active. Apply the Angled Strokes filter, but this time with the Direction Balance pushed to 100.

7, 8 In the Layers palette, make all three layers visible and change the blending mode of the filtered layers. There are many possibilities—here both layers are changed to Screen blending mode for a light and ethereal effect.

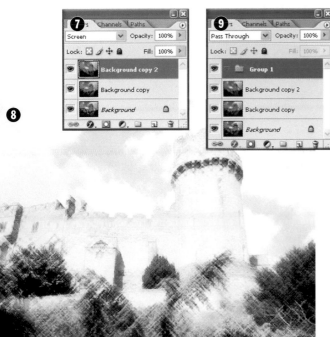

Crosshatch STROKES

Crosshatch is a close cousin to Angled Strokes, but with equal emphasis in each stroke direction. The filter has the advantage over real artists' cross-hatching, in that individual strokes are composed of different colors because they react to the underlying image.

How it works

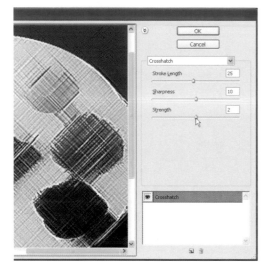

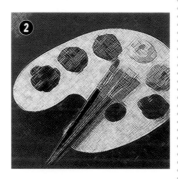

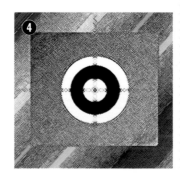

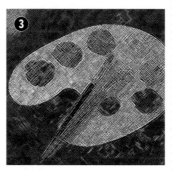

1 Medium settings of Stroke Length 25, Sharpness 10, and Strength 2 produce an over-strong result on this small original.

2 Decreasing Stroke Length to 10 and increasing Sharpness to 20 produces an interesting "knitted" effect.

3 With both Sharpness and Strength at maximum, the image is attacked on all fronts, and is perhaps a little too abstract to be useful.

4 At the same settings, the target image shows how this filter introduces spectral noise effects in gray areas.

Using the Crosshatch filter

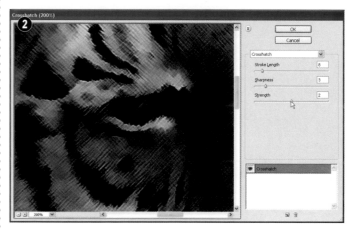

This simple technique applies Crosshatch in increments, in conjunction with Image > Adjustments > Hue/Saturation.

1, 2 Apply the Crosshatch filter with Stroke Length 8, Sharpness 3, and Strength 2.

3 Choose the Lasso tool and set it to a soft feather of about 20 pixels in the Tool Options bar.

4 Select all (Ctrl/Cmd+A), hold down the Alt/Option key and use the Lasso tool to subtract a small area from the overall selection. When the subtraction is complete, hit Ctrl/Cmd+F to re-apply the filter at the same settings.

5 With the selection still active, go to **Image > Adjustments > Hue/ Saturation** and reduce the saturation of the selected area. We took this initial selection down to -24.

6 Once again, use the Lasso tool with the Alt/Option key depressed to further reduce the selection. Reapply the Crosshatch filter (Ctrl/ Cmd+F) then reduce saturation as before.

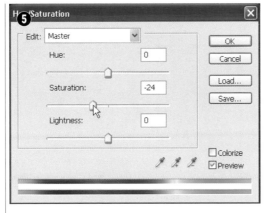

7 Continue subtracting from the selection, reapplying the filter and desaturating until only the last active area remains. The effect is a gradual increase in color up to the focal point of the image—the tiger's face.

Ink Outlines

The Ink Outlines filter offers an interesting "drawn" line effect in combination with a background mottling that recalls the Sponge filter (see page 15).

How it works

1 Set to Stroke Length 7, Dark Intensity 5, Light Intensity 5, a fine line (always black, irrespective of palette settings) traces color and tone edges. Mottled patterns can be seen in the balance of the image and, in close-up, some vestigial cross-hatching can be seen in the highlight areas.

2 The Stroke Length control is curiously named. Setting it to maximum (50) has the effect of spreading highlights and displacing the traced line—compare this close-up with the previous example.

3 A useful compromise setting (15, 5, and 50) gives a more effective result that's lighter and not so emphatically mottled.

4 The same settings applied to the target image show the line displacement. Note the metallic effect that has appeared over the area of gray gradation.

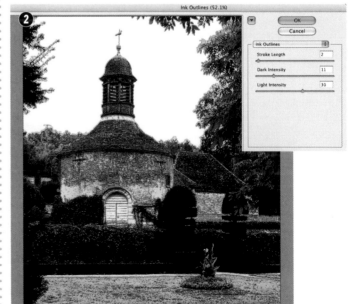

Using the Ink Outlines filter

You can use Ink Outlines as a remedy to breathe some life into otherwise flat subjects.

1, 2 Duplicate the original image in the Layers palette and apply the Ink Outlines filter. Keep the Stroke Length low to avoid overpowering the original image. Here, the values that we have used are Stroke Length 2, Dark Intensity 11, and Light Intensity 30.

3, 4, 5 Even at a low setting such as this, the effect is too strong. Use **Edit > Fade > Ink Outlines** to restrain it.

6 In close-up, it's easy to see the reviving effect of the filter.

Fixing color cast with Ink Outlines

Another rescue mission involves mitigating irreversible color casts.

1 A heavy cast due to fluorescent lighting, with no corrective filtration at the moment of shooting, can still be sidestepped.

2 Select the whole of the image (Ctrl/Cmd+A) and copy it (Ctrl/Cmd+C). Open the Channels palette, make a new channel, and paste (Ctrl/Cmd+V) the image into it. The channel window will now show the pasted image in monochrome.

3 Use the Ink Outlines filter at low values: Stroke Length 2, Dark Intensity 14, and Light Intensity 26.

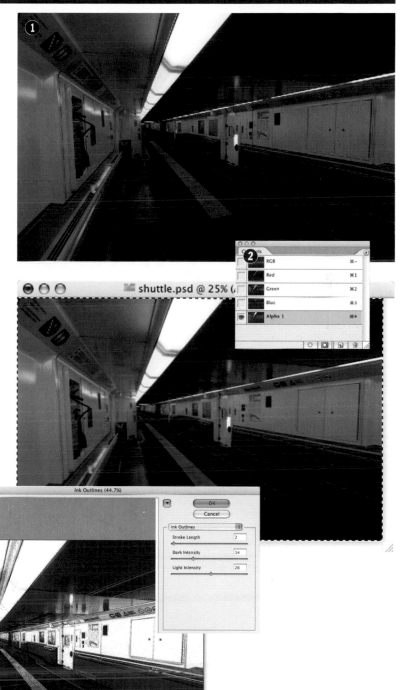

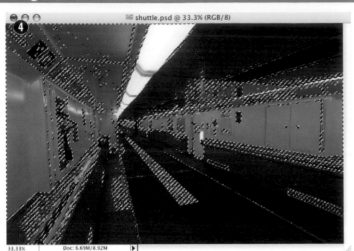

4 Hold down the Ctrl/Cmd key and click in the alpha channel thumbnail. Return to the Layers palette where the original image will show the alpha channel selection. Hide the selection (Ctrl/Cmd+H) so that the work area is easier to see.

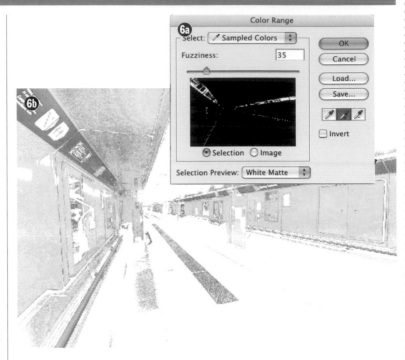

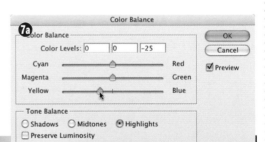

7a, 7b Use Image Adjustments > Color Balance (Ctrl/Cmd+B), uncheck Preserve Luminosity and increase the yellow component in Highlight, Midtone and Shadow areas. When you're done, click OK and then Ctrl/Cmd+D to deselect. The handrails and warning panels are now much closer in color to the original.

5a, 5b Use Image > Adjustments > Brightness/Contrast to lighten, and reduce the color strength of, the selected areas.

6a, 6b Though the correction is acceptable, more detailed work can pay dividends. The originally bright yellow warning panels and handrails are now pink. Click the Eyedropper tool in a typical pink area and go to Select > Color Range. Select the central eyedropper icon to add more related colors to the selection by clicking in the main image window. Choose White Matte as the Selection Preview from time to time to check progress. When satisfied, click OK.

66

Spatter

To introduce a lightly rippled effect, use the Spatter filter. Pixels are displaced in all directions, with the distance of displacement controlled by the Spray Radius slider. On its own, this offers a rather jagged result, which application of the Smoothness slider can remedy. This is a quicker route, though rather one-dimensional compared with the more complex Displace and Glass filters in the Distort menu (see pages 74 and 76 respectively).

How it works

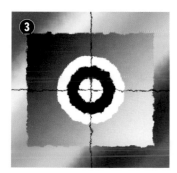

1 At mid-settings of Spray Radius 13, Smoothness 8, the image begins to break up.

2 At maximum settings, the result is reminiscent of very nervous painting.

3 This is confirmed by the same settings used on the target image.

Using the Spatter filter

This technique offers a quick route to a simulated aquatint effect using two adjacent filters in the Brush Strokes suite.

1 The original image is a depressing rain-lashed view from the interior of a Scottish art school.

2 Duplicate the original in the Layers palette and apply the Ink Outlines filter to the new layer using values Stroke Length 16, Dark Intensity 23, and Light Intensity 26.

3 Hide the filtered layer and make the original layer active. Apply the Spatter filter at maximum

4, 5 Activate the top layer and change its blending mode to Linear Dodge to give a bright, grainy effect.

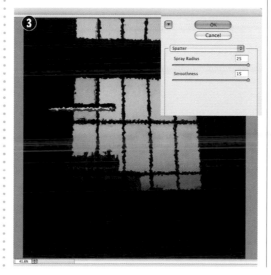

Sprayed Strokes

A useful simulation combining a painterly effect with controlled distortion, Sprayed Strokes benefits from a direction control (the only one in the Brush Strokes suite). Compare this filter with Angled Strokes (page 62) to see the difference that this makes. Try this filter in combination with one of the blur filters to soften its effect.

How it works

1 Low settings of Stroke Length 2, Spray Radius 3, and Stroke Direction Left Diagonal give a moderately frantic result.

2 Although high values of Stroke Length (here with Horizontal selected as Stroke Direction) can be useful, the Spray Radius needs to be kept low to avoid destroying the image.

Using the Sprayed Strokes filter

This filter is most useful when firmed up with other effects. In this case the trusty Emboss filter is pressed into service.

1, 2 Duplicate the image twice in the Layers palette.

3, 4 Go to **Filter > Sketch > Emboss** and apply a small pixel height of 10. an angle of 150°, and a percentage of 100. Hit OK. Change the layer blending mode to Pin Light, hide this layer and work on the next layer down.

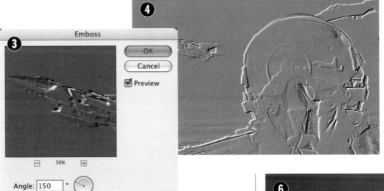

5, 6 Use the Sprayed Strokes filter at maximum strength on this layer.

7 Change the layer blending mode to Exclusion, reduce its opacity to 75%, and then make all layers visible to see the final effect.

68

Sumi-e

In Japanese, sumi-e means "black ink painting"—by implication, black ink on a white ground. The act of painting is preceded by around 25 minutes of ink-grinding, time that is also used for contemplation. The skilled painter produces strokes of greatly differing widths during one pass of the brush. The Photoshop filter attempts to simulate such brushwork with a slider each for Stroke Width and Stroke Pressure. The inherently high contrast effect of the filter can be further increased with the third slider.

How it works

1 At minimum settings there is already a blurring effect.

2 You'll need to juggle the sliders to avoid over-filling the image with black. These settings manage to retain some of the original detail.

3, 4 A monochrome image makes a better starting point, treated at the same settings as step 2.

5 Once again at the same settings, the target image confirms that the brush effect operates most strongly on hard edges, much less so on soft gradations such as those between the spectral colors.

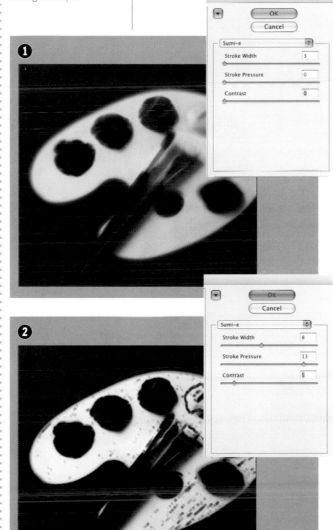

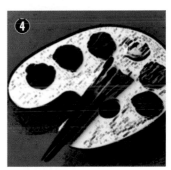

The Distort filters

Some of Photoshop's most powerful filters reside in the Distort suite. Except for Diffuse Glow, they all work by displacing pixels. Although all of the filters in the suite come with preset displacement maps and textures, you can also create your own for use with the Displace and Glass filters. For really dynamic effects, give Ripple, Shear, Twirl, or ZigZag a try. Application of the Ocean Ripple filter gives a gentler, textured result. If you are looking for more geometric distortions, try Pinch, Polar Coordinates, or Spherize. And, for complete destruction of your original image, you can take full advantage of the seven sliders and three modes of Wave.

The Distort filters

page 71—Ocean Ripple

page 72—Diffuse Glow

page 74—Displace

page 76—Glass

page 78—Lens Correction

page 80—Ripple

page 81—ZigZag

page 82—Pinch

page 84—Polar Coordinates

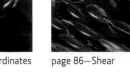

page 86—Shear

page 88—Spherize

page 89—Twirl

page 90—Wave

Ocean Ripple

Ocean Ripple is a close cousin of the Glass filter (see page 76), but it makes use of a random pattern rather than the set distortion patterns of the Glass filter.

How it works

1 Choosing 3 for Ripple Size and 7 for Magnitude gives a slightly impasto appearance.

2 Pushing both sliders to their maximum—Ripple Size 15, Ripple Magnitude 20—gives a painterly effect reminiscent of Klimt.

3 The target image at the same settings shows the slightly square ripples that are produced when this filter is pushed to its maximum.

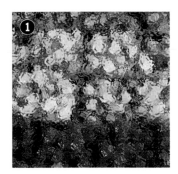

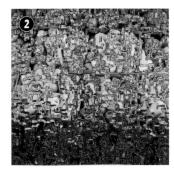

Using the Ocean Ripple filter

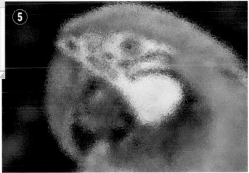

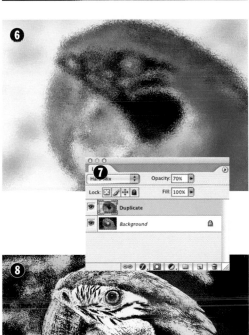

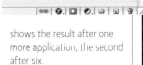

Progressive applications of the Ocean Ripple filter can provide an overlay for the source image.

1, 2 Duplicate the original layer by dragging on to the "turned page" icon in the Layers palette.

3 Apply the Ocean Ripple filter at medium intensity (Ripple Size 7, Ripple Magnitude 11).

4, 5 Continue applying the filter using the same settings—the first image shows the result after one more application, the second after six.

6 Invert the upper layer (**Image > Adjustments > Invert** or just hit Ctrl/Cmd+I).

7, 8 Set the blending mode of the active layer to Hard Mix and its opacity to 70%.

Diffuse Glow

The Diffuse Glow filter adds a soft glow to an image, and attempts to do so more in the background than over the main subject. The highlight color depends on the background color in the Toolbox palette, with the default white usually being the most successful. The filter works well on portraits, and can be used as an alternative to the clichéd soft focus effect.

How it works

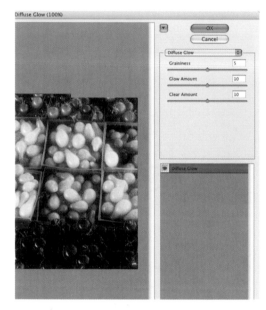

1 At medium settings of Graininess 5, Glow Amount 10, Clear Amount 10, Diffuse Glow adds a layer of grain and spreads the highlights.

2 Anything other than the default white will tint the highlights—as in this grim example with the palette background color changed to bright green.

3 Though a failure on vegetables, Diffuse Glow has a role in softening portraits. With background color reset to white, settings of Graininess 8, Glow Amount 13, and Clear Amount 10 give a reasonable simulation of a grainy high-key color portrait.

Using the Diffuse Glow filter

To extend the "high key" look in this photo of a young woman, you need to vary the effect of the Diffuse Glow filter.

1, 2, 3 The original gains an ethereal effect from an overall application at medium strength, but the already flat single-bulb lighting is flattened further.

4, 5 Take a step back and discard the filtered version. Duplicate the original layer in the Layers palette, apply the original filter settings to the copied layer, and change its blending mode to Pin Light at around 80%.

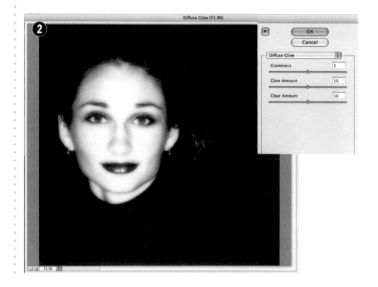

6 The combined layers retain the glow effect, but with much better modeling.

Careful choice of palette background color can produce mysterious effects.

1, 2 Click in the background part of the color palette to activate the Color Picker. In this case a complementary color to the overall blue is selected. This color will be automatically introduced to the filtered image.

3, 4 The Clear Amount slider is the most important control to avoid drowning the image in glop. Values of Graininess 6, Glow Amount 7, and Clear Amount 11 were used here.

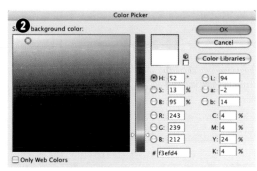

Displace

Displace is a powerful and yet subtle method of shifting pixels. It's well worth experimenting to become familiar with its possibilities. The vital component of Displace is a Displacement Map, sometimes referred to as a dmap. Try applying the filter at varying settings to a pattern of black-and-white stripes to get a Bridget Riley effect—this is a good demonstration of how the filter works.

How it works

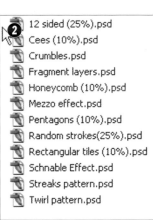

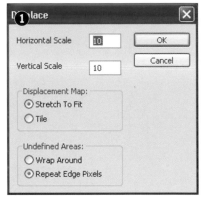

1 The initial dialog box requests input for Horizontal and Vertical Scale, how the map is to be applied, and how the inevitable missing edge areas are to be filled. Choose 10 (the default setting) for Horizontal and Vertical Scale, check Stretch to Fit and Repeat Edge Pixels. Click OK to go to the next stage.

2 The built-in list of displacement maps will appear in a window. If the maps don't appear, you'll need to navigate to the Photoshop application folder—the Displacement Maps folder is inside the Plug-Ins folder.

3 Choose 12-sided from the list and hit OK. The result shows a slight distortion.

4 For a more emphatic effect, choose 40 for both Horizontal and Vertical Scale.

5 With the same settings, but with Tiling selected, the effect is totally different, with the pentagons now acting as tiny lenses.

6 Substituting the target image and choosing Cees, the filter has an explosive effect.

7 With Twirl, the image dissolves into curling shapes.

8 The supplied displacement maps themselves are ordinary RGB Photoshop files. They are small compared to the images that they will usually be used to treat—the Pentagon map for example is only 28 pixels square, with values in the red and green channels only.

9 The red channel is for horizontal displacement, and the green for vertical. The blue channel is not significant (and neither is the composite RGB channel). The "color" of each channel is not significant either—the filter just looks at the grayscale values of the first two available channels in the displacement map.

Light areas in the first channel push pixels to the left, while dark areas push them to the right. In the second channel, light areas push up, and dark areas push down. The shifting of an individual pixel is therefore influenced by the brightness, or lack of it, in both channels. The distance shifted can then be controlled by the Scale settings in the dialog box.

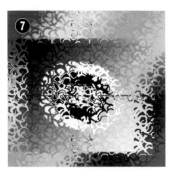

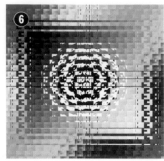

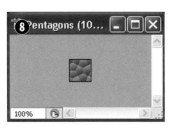

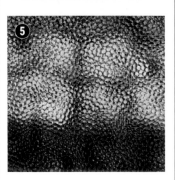

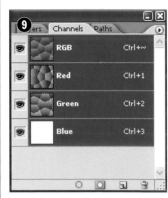

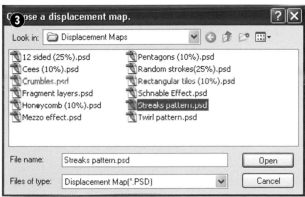

You can make use of the Fade feature to emphasize the effect of Displace.

1, 2 The crisp, clean lines of this brandy glass will make a good counterpoint to the chaotic effect of the Displace filter. Run Displace, and increase the default scale of 10 to 35 for a more extreme effect. Click OK.

3, 4 Navigate to the Displacement Maps folder, choose the Streaks option and click Open.

5, 6 Immediately go to the **Edit** > **Fade Displace** menu, choose Difference as the blending mode, and reduce the opacity of the filtration to around 50%.

Glass

This filter can make your pictures look as if they are being viewed through textured glass. The filter uses the same displacement map fundamentals as Displace but expressed in a different form, with the luxury of a preview window and a more intuitive interface. Load Textures brings up a window to select your own textures, but you can just as easily experiment with six of the 12 Photoshop displacement maps used in Displace. The six maps that appear grayed-out in the dialog—Crumbles, Fragment layers, Mezzo effect, Schnable effect, Streaks pattern, and Twirl pattern—are ancient souvenirs of Photoshop 2.0 and are still saved in that format. Just open them separately and re-save (and re-name if you like) in your current version of Photoshop. They will then be available to the Glass filter.

How it works

1 Set Distortion and Smoothness to medium, choose Frosted from the Textures menu, and leave Scaling at 100% as a starting point.

2 Try again with Blocks selected and you'll see, paradoxically, a more curvaceous result.

3 Increase the Distortion value to near maximum (here, it's 9) and the pixels begin to stir vigorously— here enlarged 200%.

4 The target image has been subjected to Distortion 5, Smoothness 3, and the Frosted texture.

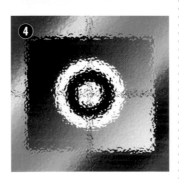

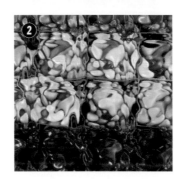

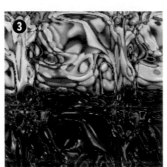

Using the Glass filter

You can augment the range of effects available in the Glass filter by using Photoshop's own folder of textures (you'll find them by navigating to Adobe Photoshop CS2 > Presets > Textures), as well as by adding your own displacement maps.

1, 2, 3 Open your image and run the Glass filter with the settings: Distortion 8, and Smoothness 11. Using one of the presets—Blocks, in this case—a mechanical result is produced.

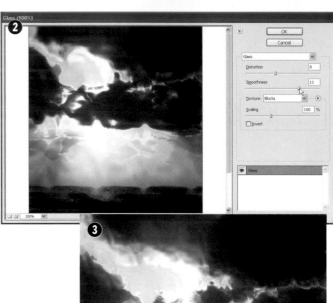

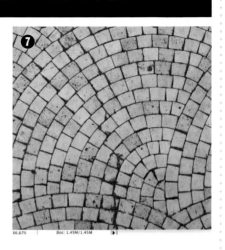

7, 8, 9 For the home-made map approach, this section of mosaic floor offers an additional opportunity—to echo shapes within the main image with the displacement map. The mosaic image is less than half the size of the main image, but this is not evident in the finished result. There's no need to put the home-made map in a particular folder to access it—jut hit Load Texture in the Glass filter window and navigate to it.

4, 5, 6 By invoking the Load Texture function (by clicking on the small arrow next to the Texture pull-down menu) you can access the standard displacement maps or the Photoshop Textures folder. Only Photoshop (.psd) files are suitable, so the others are grayed-out. In this case the Frosted Glass texture was applied at an enlargement of 125% for a coarser effect. By the way, it's immaterial whether the Photoshop file is color or monochrome.

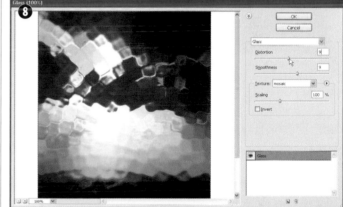

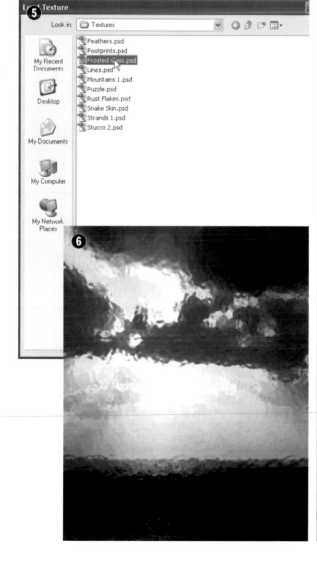

Lens Correction

The Lens Correction filter introduced in CS2 consolidates some existing effects and adds a couple of features that prove very useful in rescuing marginal pictures. As the name suggests, the purpose of the filter is to correct aberrations, such as pincushioning, that may occur with an incorrectly set lens.

How it works

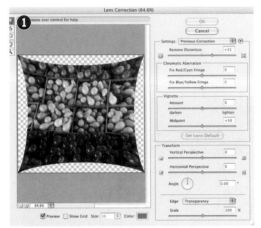

1 The large panel has a toolbox that duplicates some of the features in the dialog boxes. For example, you can draw freehand over the image with the Remove Distortion tool, and the change is reflected in the matching slider on the right side of the panel.

2a, 2b The next tool, Straighten, allows you to re-orient the image. Click and drag along the proposed new axis, and when you release the mouse, the image will swing around. Incidentally, the Angle icon on the right side of the main panel gives a precise readout of the changed orientation.

3 In the previous examples, the grid pattern has been switched off to show the tools more clearly. It is visible by default, and the third tool allows you to drag it around over the image if you need more precise placement. The final two tools, Hand and Zoom, act in the same way as they do in a normal Photoshop document.

4 Moving to the sliders area, Chromatic Aberration offers a fix for color fringing, while Vignette darkens or lightens the periphery of the image.

5 Perspective control is familiar from the **Edit > Transform** menu, but in this filter, vertical and horizontal perspective can be invoked simultaneously.

6 Try Vertical and Horizontal Perspective together with an alteration in the Angle value, and add Edge Extension with a diminution in the scale of the source image for a surprising result.

7 For the sake of completeness, here's the long-suffering target image treated with almost maximum values on all of the sliders.

Using the Lens Correction filter

The Lens Correction filter can be used for correcting poorly-shot images as well as problems with the camera lens itself.

1 This original has been shot off-axis, and also suffers from barrel distortion attributable to a poorly corrected lens. It's a perfect target for the Lens Correction filter. We'll use the Perspective sliders and the Angle control to fix the faulty geometry, and the Remove Distortion slider to try and remove the barreling effect.

2 The first thing to do is to ensure the grid is visible by checking the Show Grid box underneath the image. This is critical in ensuring that everything is aligned properly.

3 With the grid visible, you can now finesse the Remove Distortion slider to cure the barreling. A value of 5 seems to fix this image.

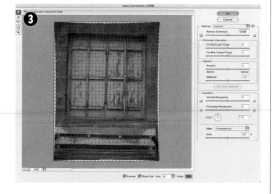

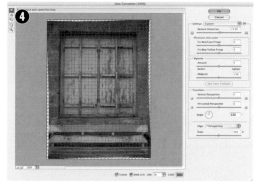

4 Next, use the Angle control to correct the vertical. Although the image seems to be leaning to the right a fair amount, it only needs a tiny adjustment to bring it back into line.

5 The image is almost ready, but, as a result of previous adjustments in combination with the original distortion, the perspective is still not quite right. This can easily be corrected with the Transform sliders. Adjust the Vertical and Horizontal Perspective to bring the image into correct alignment with the grid.

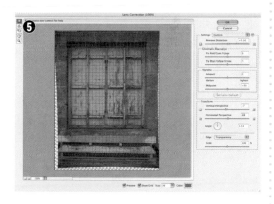

6 Inevitably, as a result of this process, the edges of the image will no longer be square. Either use the Crop tool to fix this, or fill the gaps with the Clone tool if the edges can be restored seamlessly.

Ripple

Not the kid brother to Ocean Ripple, but another iteration of the texture map technique. The controls offer a slider running from −999% to +999% (though the effects are rather similar irrespective of whether you choose the positive or negative route), and a Small/Medium/Large choice of waveform.

How it works

1 At settings of Amount -500, Size Medium, the image breaks into agitated arabesques—if thoroughly blurred it would make a pleasant background for another subject.

2 Choose Small and set the slider at -350 for a somewhat stroked appearance (enlarged to show the detail).

3 Finally, the target suffers here under the influence of Large ripples at 999%.

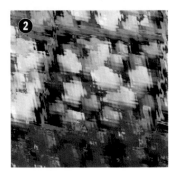

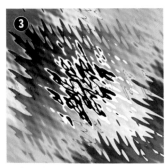

Using the Ripple filter

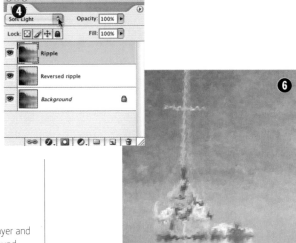

For more control, try the Wave filter (see page 90), but for low-impact shimmering, stick with Ripple.

1, 2 Open the document and duplicate the original layer by dragging the thumbnail image onto the "turned page" icon at the foot of the Layers palette. Run the Ripple filter with Small for Size, at 500%.

3 Hide the filtered layer and activate the background layer. Choose Select All (Ctrl/Cmd+A) and go to **Edit > Transform > Flip Horizontal.** Apply the filter again at the same settings—just hit Ctrl/Cmd+F. Go again to **Edit > Transform > Flip Horizontal** to restore the image to its original orientation.

4, 5, 6 Change the blending mode of the upper layer to Soft Light to reveal the "woven" quality that has been produced in conjunction with the lower layer.

ZigZag

A close relative of the Glass filter, ZigZag offers an effective pond ripple effect. With Ridges set to 1, the different Style settings can emulate the effects of the Pinch and Twirl filters, but ZigZag really comes into its own when a larger number of Ridges is employed.

How it works

1 Pond Ripple, as its name suggests, resembles the ripples created when a stone is thrown into a pond. Here Amount is set to 30, and Ridges to 5.

2 Selecting Around Center in the Style popup introduces a second wave pattern.

3 The Out From Center style needs more aggressive settings (60 and 15 respectively) to achieve an equally strong effect.

Using the ZigZag filter

Now for a little stunt flying. Disengage all safety features and duplicate the original image layer.

1 Choose the Elliptical Marquee tool, click and drag out from the center of the propeller while holding down the Alt/Option and Shift keys.

2 Apply the ZigZag filter with both values at maximum, and Style set to Pond Ripples.

You can preview the effect in the dialog box. Hit OK, then Deselect (Ctrl/Cmd+D).

3 Apply the same procedure to the second aircraft, and then Deselect.

4 Change the blending mode of the upper layer to Color. Invert the color values of the upper layer (Ctrl/Cmd+I), then duplicate this treated layer.

5, 6 Change the blending mode of the new layer to Linear Burn and reduce its opacity to 60%.

7 Duplicate the Linear Burn layer, change its blending mode to Color Burn, and set its opacity to 35%.

8, 9 To get that almost authentic Roy Lichtenstein feel, go to **Filter > Pixelate > Color Halftone** and apply the settings shown to the Color Burn layer.

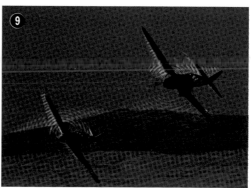

Pinch

Although the name of this filter only refers to pinch, this filter also controls its opposite, punch. The companion filter, Spherize, offers more flexibility and a sharper edge, but the Pinch filter will suffice for simple circular distortions.

How it works

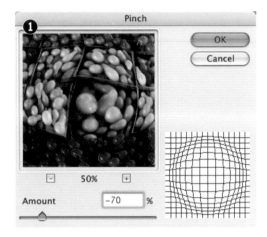

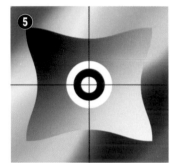

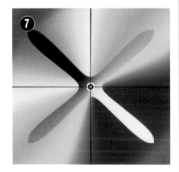

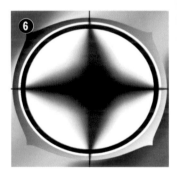

1, 2 One slider controls the effect, giving, at negative values, a "punch" result in which the central area balloons out. Even at this small scale it's clear that there is a loss of sharpness in the distorted area.

3 Move the slider to a positive value, 70 in this case, and the center of the image retreats. Now the loss of definition can be seen on the periphery of the "dish" area. In both examples it would be wise to start with a high-resolution photograph to combat this inevitable degradation.

4 The target image shows the effect of the same settings even more clearly.

5, 6, 7 Repeating the filter leads to curious results.

Descend for a moment, if you will, into the murky world of pattern-making.

1, 2, 3 A shot of an airport terminal skylight provides sufficient symmetry for this exercise. Duplicate the background layer by dragging the thumbnail on to the "turned page" icon in the Layers palette, and apply the Pinch filter at full strength.

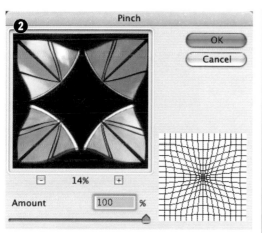

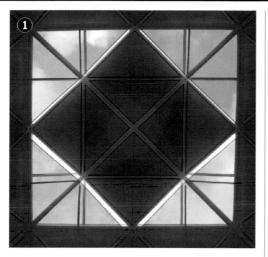

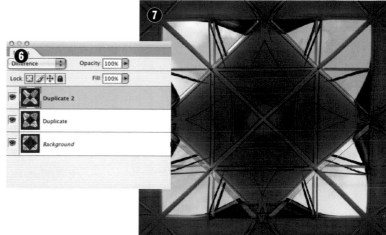

4, 5 Change the blending mode of the filtered duplicate layer to Difference.

6, 7, 8 Now duplicate this filtered and mode-changed layer, and immediately hit Ctrl/Cmd+F to apply the Pinch filter again.

9 Keep on repeating the process—duplicate the layer, re-apply the filter, duplicate the layer, and so on—until you achieve a pleasing image. Here's the result of a four-deep layer stack.

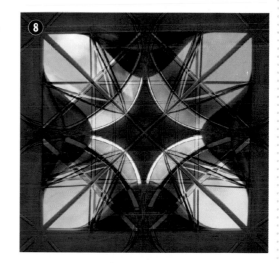

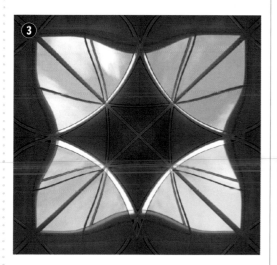

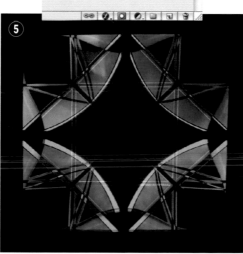

Shear

Shear distorts an image along a user-defined curve, and its possibilities are only limited by your persistence in drawing and re-drawing that curve in the command window. If you're familiar with a vector-based drawing program like Illustrator or Freehand, you'll recognize the way the curve responds to the addition of extra points. The result can be taken to extremes by constant repetition of the filter. The filter offers two methods of filling the otherwise empty spaces that are created when it's run. Wrap Around simply makes any pixels that move out of frame on one side of the image appear on the other, and Repeat Edge Pixels stretches out the final line of pixels at the edge of the image to fill the gap. Which one you choose depends very much on your original image—Wrap Around works best when the sides of the image are similar to each other, and Repeat Edge Pixels works best when the edges are made up of simple areas of flat color. See the following example for more correction techniques.

How it works

1, 2, 3, 4 Check Wrap Around, click on the graph line and drag the points to a new position using the simple grid to get a symmetrical result.

5 Repeat Edge Pixels produces streaks at the image edges that are extremely noticeable in detailed images such as this.

6 A more useful feature is sometimes overlooked. Click on Defaults to return the

graph to a straight vertical line, and then drag the top and bottom points in opposite directions .

7 The sloping effect can add interest to photographs originally shot straight on and, conversely, can be used to a limited extent to correct shots which are skewed in the camera.

8 Here's the target image showing Repeat Edge Pixels working on flat color.

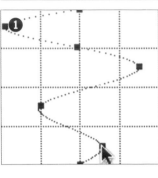

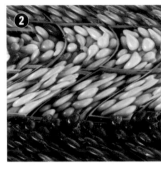

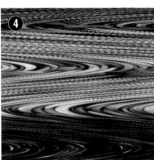

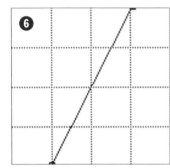

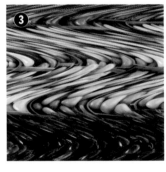

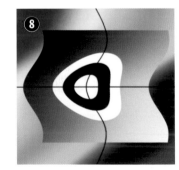

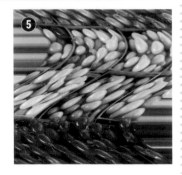

Though it's tempting to compose crazy curves in the Shear filter, better results are to be had by enhancing pre-existing features in the source picture.

1, 2 Open the Shear filter, click to add one point on the vertical line, and drag it to the ledt. Drag the top and bottom points to the right, check Repeat Edge pixels, and click OK.

3 The result successfully emphasizes the sweeping curves of the original—but the repeated edge pixels, especially at the right side, need correction, so draw a rectangular marquee to enclose the area.

4, 5 Open the Liquify filter (in the top section of the Filter menu) and choose the topmost tool in the toolbox (the Forward Warp tool). If you have a pressure-sensitive stylus setup, check the Stylus Pressure checkbox. Use the Forward Warp tool by clicking and dragging in the intended direction of the revised curve. There is only one

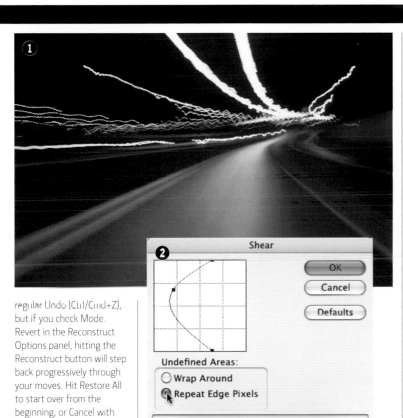

1

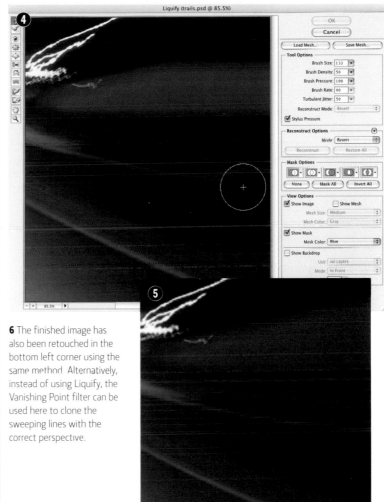

Shear

Undefined Areas:
- ○ Wrap Around
- ● Repeat Edge Pixels

OK
Cancel
Defaults

regular Undo (Ctrl/Cmd+Z), but if you check Mode: Revert in the Reconstruct Options panel, hitting the Reconstruct button will step back progressively through your moves. Hit Restore All to start over from the beginning, or Cancel with the Alt/Option key pressed to get a reset. Also try the Bloat tool to enlarge the image if necessary. After several attempts, the area should begin to match the general curves, if not, just crop off the right side of the image and forget it.

6 The finished image has also been retouched in the bottom left corner using the same method. Alternatively, instead of using Liquify, the Vanishing Point filter can be used here to clone the sweeping lines with the correct perspective.

3

6

Spherize

Spherize differs from Pinch in its more sharply defined slope to the globe shape. The panel offers the same negative-to-positive slider and a choice of distortion in both axes at once (named Normal), or Horizontal or Vertical only.

How it works

1 At settings of Amount 80, Mode Normal, an effective spherical distortion results, but suffers from softness as the pixels are stretched.

2 Negative values give a progressively concave result.

3, 4 Bear in mind that a globe is produced only when treating a square image. If you start with a rectangular picture, then you'll get an elliptical result.

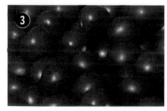

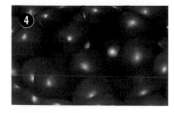

Using the Spherize filter

The Spherize filter can be used to create effective water droplets.

1, 2 Choose the Elliptical Marquee tool and set its Feather radius in the menu bar to around 3 pixels. Hold down Shift and draw a small circle marquee. Go to the Spherize filter and choose the minimum value—perversely, the inverse sphere seems to give better results. Click OK.

3, 4 Choose the Burn tool from the toolbox and set its Brush Tip to minimum hardness and a diameter of 250 pixels.

5 Click and drag with the Burn tool to darken the upper left edge of the selection to give it the appearance of being 3D.

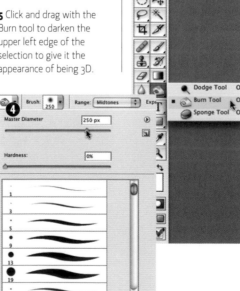

6 Hold down the Alt/Option key (this turns the Burn tool into the Lighten tool) and treat the lower right edge of the selection.

7 Continue in this way—filter, burn, lighten—until exhaustion sets in. You'll need to deselect (Ctrl/Cmd+D) in between each droplet, otherwise the Shift key won't constrain the marquee tool to a circle.

Twirl

irst there was Twirl, then, years later, Liquify (see page 182) arrived and supercharged the business of spinning, smearing, and ultimately exploding the photographic image. There is only a single slider that controls the Twirl filter: positive Angle values give a right-hand twirl, while negative values give a left-hand one.

How it works

1 Try a small Angle for a gentle introduction.

2 For a more extreme effect, either increase the Angle setting, or simply repeat the filter several times, as here (use Ctrl/Cmd+F to repeat the filter with the same settings).

3 Negative angle settings reverse the direction of the twirl effect.

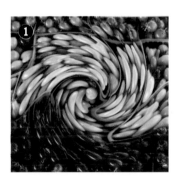

Using the Twirl filter

A very little Twirl might be beneficial from time to time, but image selection is all important.

1, 2, 3 Pictures with a simple rotational dynamic can be enhanced with slight distortion. Try a low value to add some drama.

4, 5 Set at 8, the effect of Twirl is almost undetectable. Raised to 20, it's still just about acceptable, but at 40, it begins to look unreal.

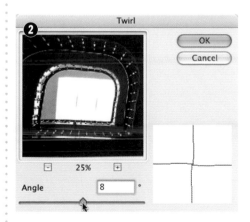

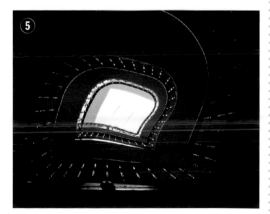

Wave

In the Wave dialog are seven sliders, three choices of waveform, and a Randomize function. Though it's the work of a moment to produce a frenzied result, a more logical approach (a sequence of manageable numbers, for example) can pay off if you're in search of a particular distortion. In particular, the number of Generators has a huge effect on the result. Try starting low with just one generator and then incrementally increase the number to see the effect before experimenting with higher values.

How it works

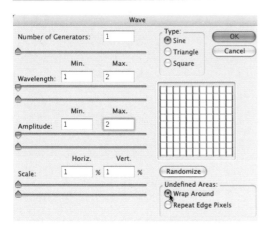

1 This square grid has been treated with a Sine curve as follows: Generators 50; Wavelength Min 75, Max 100; Amplitude Min 125, Max 150; with the Scale left at just 1% in both axes. At these settings, the grid responds with a recognizably sinuous wave effect.

2 With an increase in Generators to 150, the curves become more extreme.

3 Increasing the Scale to 5% in both axes produces a violent switchback motion.

4 Increasing the maximum value of Amplitude to 500 breaks up the regular pattern entirely.

5 Continual repetition of the filter will eventually give a moiré effect.

6, 7 Try all these maneuvers with the Triangle and Square alternatives and, for good measure, invoke the Randomize button as well. For the record, here are the photographic and color targets treated with the same values as step 4.

8 Using the Square curve type and altering the settings to Generators 100, Min. Wavelength 588, Max. Wavelength 589, Min. Amplitude 129, Max. Amplitude 815, Horiz. Scale 60, Vert. Scale 13 and Wrap Around gives an interesting displaced version.

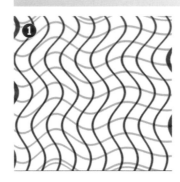

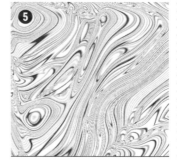

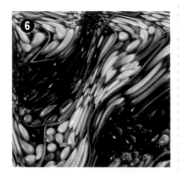

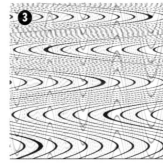

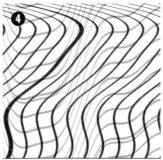

The Wave filter, perhaps unsurprisingly, lends itself well to images based on water. This swimmer is a perfect example.

1, 2, 3 Push the Number of Generators slider to its maximum, and Wavelength and Amplitude to their minimum. The Scale sliders influence the degree of destruction of the original, and have been set here to minimize it. The filter effect has also been faded (**Edit > Fade Wave**) to 60% with Normal blend to allow the original to show through.

4, 5 A more conservative setting of the Number of Generators value, mid-range for Wavelength with low Amplitude, and maximum Scale in both axes, gives a multiple image, Checking Repeat Pixels causes the streaking in between the images. Try the Randomize button to cycle through a number of variations.

6, 7 With a solitary generator you have more control over the distortion. The more difference between the Wavelength sliders, the more destruction; the same is true for the Amplitude control. Again, use the Randomize button repeatedly to find a pleasing result.

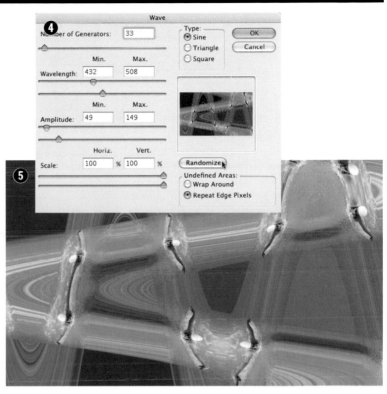

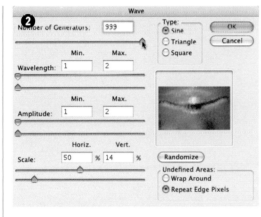

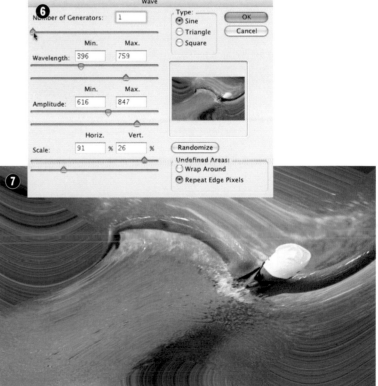

The Noise filters

"Image noise" is a term borrowed from audio. Interference that disturbs the pure sound signal generates noise. Though the sound engineer and photographer usually both struggle to reduce noise, the photographer may on occasion want to increase it. Photoshop CS2's four Noise filters can be used to either add or reduce image noise. The Add Noise filter, for example, can help to redeem pictures where shadows and/or highlights have become too intense, by adding texture to the offending areas. This filter is equally useful in "restoring" to digital images the characteristic film grain of a conventional silver-based emulsion. Despeckle, as the name suggests, reduces image noise. It's a blunt instrument with no user settings, but can succeed on a case-by-case basis. It works by blurring pixels area-wide, but doesn't affect edge areas. Dust & Scratches is a more sophisticated tool that can operate as a generalized fix for scanned images that show a moderate amount of dust or damage. It's also a useful first stage in rescuing more seriously damaged photographs, which will subsequently need localized retouching. The Median filter looks for adjacent pixels of dissimilar brightness and deletes them in favor of new pixels that average the surrounding values. Last, yet possibly most useful, the new Reduce Noise filter goes directly to the heart of digital degradation—it removes unwanted noise and the crude artifacts produced by overdoing image compression in the JPEG format.

The Noise filters

page 93—Despeckle

page 94—Add Noise

page 96—Dust & Scratches

page 98—Reduce Noise

page 101—Median

Despeckle

This filter has no user settings, but can have a beneficial effect on images compromised by noise as well as other unwanted artifacts. It works by finding edge areas in an image and blurring everything but those edge areas. In this way, detail in the image is preserved, while areas of speckled color are smoothed out.

How it works

1 In this magnified example, the shadow area shows the typical noise effect that is often produced in digital images that are taken at high ISO/ASA ratings.

2 One application of the Despeckle filter can help significantly in this area—try repeated applications, but retreat when the image begins to soften unacceptably.

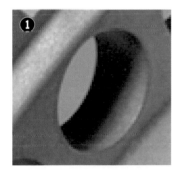

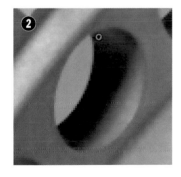

Amount: 15 %
Radius: 4 pixels
Threshold: 20 levels

9 A direct before (left) and after (right) comparison of the image shows that the process has smoothed it considerably, and removed some of the artefacts that were present. However, it has also removed a lot of detail. This isn't such a problem with the background wall, but the paving is unacceptably soft.

Despeckle can be used to fix moiré patterns resulting from optical interference (in silk fabric, for example) and to disguise the dot structure in already screened printed pictures.

1 The closeup shows a section of the original transparency.

2 The resulting 4-color print illustrates the characteristic rosette pattern.

3, 4 Using the Despeckle filter alone does not produce a usable result. Here are the results of two, and ten, applications of the filter.

5 A better strategy is to administer a one-pixel Gaussian Blur, and then apply Despeckle once ...

6 ... or twice.

7,8 Finally, apply the Unsharp Mask filter (Filter > Sharpen > Unsharp Mask) to try to bring back some of the clarity of the original.

Add Noise

It's curious that a little artificial noise goes a long way towards restoring a "natural" look to retouched or over-enhanced originals. Though the Amount slider runs all the way to 400%, a setting of 50% is about the maximum useful value. The distribution values control the look of the noise, with Uniform, as you'd expect, giving a more even result than Gaussian. Adding noise to a montage can help to tie all of the separate elements together.

How it works

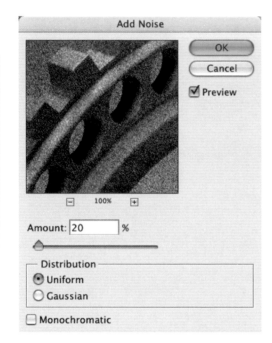

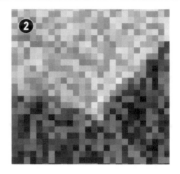  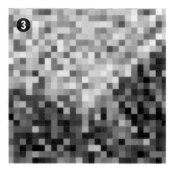

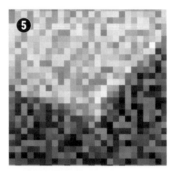  

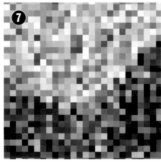  

 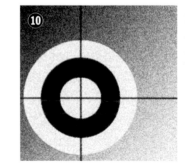 

1 Choose a low Amount value of 20% and Uniform Distribution with Monochromatic unchecked to achieve a relatively unobtrusive result.

2 The original image (here shown greatly magnified) has been covered in a randomly generated carpet of colored pixels.

3 Compare this with the result of the same settings but with Gaussian Distribution selected. You can clearly see the more speckled effect that Gaussian distribution typically produces.

4, 5 Try checking Monochrome (and reverting to Uniform distribution) for a radically different effect. In this case, the distribution of new pixels is influenced by the tone rather than the color of the originals.

6, 7 The Gaussian alternative again shows a brighter and more speckled appearance.

8, 9 Grayscale images can also benefit from a scattering of noise. Here, we've used 20%, but grayscale images can often take more noise than their color counterparts.

10 The target image, treated at 20% Uniform Distribution, shows the random choice of color in this enlargement of the gray area.

You can tone down areas of blown-out highlights with the Add Noise filter.

1, 2 This extreme example has more blown highlights than image. You'll need to use a combination of three keys: Ctrl/Cmd+Alt/Option+Tilde (~) to select the image areas which have more than 50% luminosity.

3 If you want to convince yourself that this obscure keystroke combination actually does what it says, then make a new document, hit D for the default palette, and use the Gradient tool to lay a tint right across it. Use the three-key combination, and you'll see the selected area occupying about half of the image.

4 Return to the main image and hit Ctrl/Cmd+Alt/Option+J to make a new layer out of the selection. Hit OK when the dialog window appears.

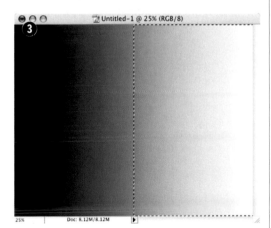

5 Ctrl/Cmd+click in the new layer thumbnail to make the selection active again.

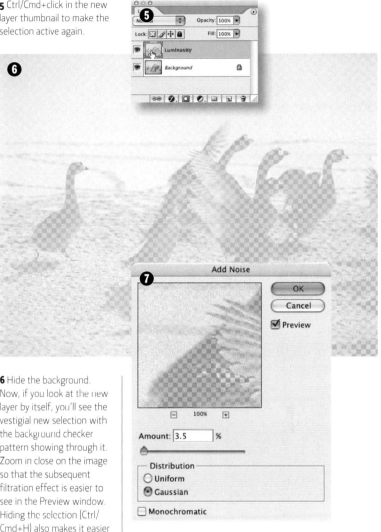

6 Hide the background. Now, if you look at the new layer by itself, you'll see the vestigial new selection with the background checker pattern showing through it. Zoom in close on the image so that the subsequent filtration effect is easier to see in the Preview window. Hiding the selection (Ctrl/Cmd+H) also makes it easier to see the effect.

7 Open the Add Noise filter and try a low value with Gaussian checked and Monochromatic unchecked.

8 The effect needs to be virtually imperceptible. In this 200% enlargement, only the right-hand side of the image is shown treated.

Dust & Scratches

This filter purports to be the film photographer's salvation, but can there really be a miracle cure for the perennial hickey? An equally common problem is how to get the filter to discern the difference between unwanted dust and hard-won detail. The sliders pull in opposite directions: Radius controls the blur amount, while Threshold limits the blur to the chosen level of detail. In practice, the best way of combining the two is to leave Threshold at 0 and then increase Radius until the defect disappears. Following that, gradually increase the Threshold, bringing detail back into the image, stopping just before the defect becomes visible again. In most cases, it is best to apply this filter only to the affected area rather than globally across the entire image. In Photoshop CS2, the Healing Brush tool in its various forms is usually a better option for eradicating major flaws than a full-strength blast of this filter. Follow it up with Dust and Scratches to take care of the lesser faults.

How it works

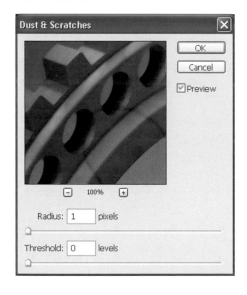

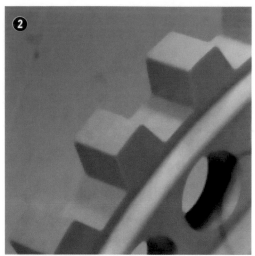

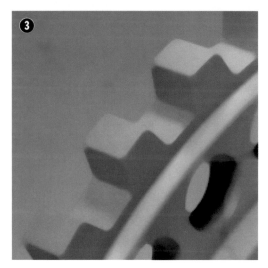
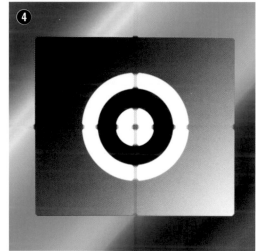

1 Here is our affected image (also shown magnified).

2 It is treated with Dust & Scratches at Radius 2, leaving Threshold set at 0. The result is a great improvement: the minor defects have been eradicated without excessively degrading the overall image.

3 However, cranking the radius up to 4 in an attempt to fix the larger faults softens the image to an unacceptable degree.

4 At Radius 4, Threshold 1, the Dust & Scratches filter has already determined that the crosshairs of our target image are blemishes that should be removed.

Secured by elegant photo corners, this black-and-white print has survived almost undamaged for about 80 years. It's not just scanned originals that gather dust, though. In the digital domain, dust can appear in certain high-specification SLRs which admit particles when lenses are being changed. These particles are attracted by the electromagnetic field surrounding the image-forming CCD and settle on its protective filter.

1, 2 In closeup, the cigar-smoker is covered in white fibers which must come from the original contact-printing process, since the modern scanner was perfectly lint-free. On the utility pole, there is later damage where the emulsion has been microscopically nicked and peeled back.

3, 4 Even at the Dust & Scratches filter's minimum setting, the effect is dramatic. The smaller fibers have disappeared altogether, though inevitably at the expense of some loss of detail in the image.

5 At a 2-pixel radius, almost all of the fibers are gone, along with a significant amount of detail.

6, 7 A useful compromise is to make a combination of 1 and 2-pixel filtration. Return to the original and duplicate it in the Layers palette. Run the filter at 1-pixel radius on the lower layer (you'll need to hide the upper layer momentarily), then activate the upper layer and run the filter at 2-pixel radius. Change the blending mode of the upper layer to Soft Light and reduce its opacity to 40%. You can add a small amount of Gaussian Blur to this layer as well to further subdue the fibers.

Reduce Noise

New in CS2, this filter promises much for the digital photographer. Noise resulting from underexposure or elevated "film speed" ratings can be reduced, and in some cases, eliminated altogether. There's also the possibility of cleaning up the characteristic block-like artifacts resulting from JPEG compression. To further finesse the noise reduction, you can treat the individual channels separately (see page 100). This facility also extends to CMYK images.

How it works

1 In order to discover the virtues of Reduce Noise, the target image has been artificially assaulted with noise, then compressed and uncompressed using JPEG.

2 A 300% enlargement shows the imperfections needing treatment.

3 The four sliders can be used independently of the Remove JPEG Artifact checkbox. You can save successful settings for future use by clicking on the tiny disk icon. The Advanced setting allows individual treatment of separate color channels.

4 At the settings shown in step 3, noise is rendered as monochromatic. There's no effect on the JPEG artifacts, since the option to remove them has not been selected.

5 With the Remove JPEG Artifact option selected, the block structure is reduced.

6, 7 Each image has its own problems, and adjusting four sliders in parallel can lead to nausea and indecision. Try increasing the overall strength of the effect using the top slider before trying increases in the other three. This combination seems a reasonable compromise between kind but incomplete rescue and all-out surgical intervention.

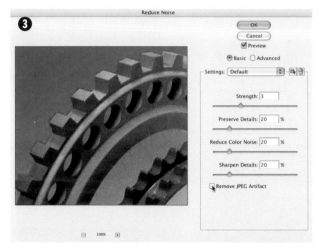

Noise is most obtrusive in the dark areas of this image—it's almost acceptable in the highlight regions.

1, 2 This setup was monitored throughout on the camera's small LCD screen and a whole day's shooting appeared to be progressing well. When the images were later transferred to the computer and viewed on a monitor, it became painfully clear that, in spite of the presence of generous amounts of studio flash equipment, the equivalent film speed had been inadvertently set to the maximum available—1600 ASA—rather than the lowest available—200 ASA.

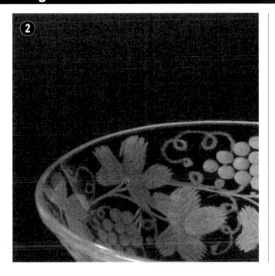

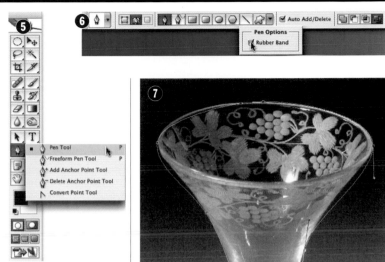

5, 6 The requirement is to confine the filter effect to the background using a mask or a selection. Given the sweeping curves of the glass, the Pen tool seems the most appropriate. In the Toolbox, the Pen tool offers several options. Choose the regular Pen tool and go to Pen presets in the contextual menu at the top of the screen. Choose Paths (the second option). The Pen tool is already the confirmed pen behavior, so click on the blue arrow to the right of the behaviors and choose Rubber Band if you're not

3 Use the Reduce Noise filter and crank the Reduce Color Noise slider to maximum. To quickly toggle between the unfiltered and filtered images, click in the preview window. The Hand tool will appear and the image will temporarily revert to its untreated state. This preview window is a montage of the two states to show the difference.

4 Moving in closer, it's clear that the filtered area (the right side of this image) has less banding and noise, but it's equally clear that the fine detail in the subject has suffered. Cancel the filter and re-consider.

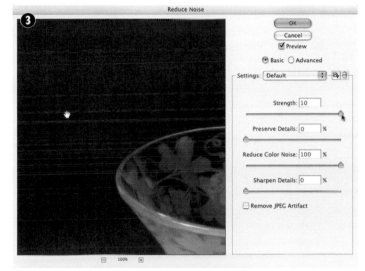

8 When the path is complete, hold down the Ctrl/Cmd key. The pen changes to an arrow that can be used to re-position points and drag handles in order to adjust curves. In general, the smoothest paths are made with the fewest points. Checking the Auto Add/Delete option allows you to delete any point on the path by clicking on it with the Pen tool.

Conversely, clicking anywhere along the line will allow you to add a point. Incidentally, holding down the Alt/Option key gives you the Convert Point tool, which will change these Smooth anchor points into Corner points.

very familiar with the tool. Checking Auto Add/Delete also makes the task easier as the pen hovers over the line in progress. The Path Areas choices at the end of the box are not significant for this operation.

7 Start drawing around the glass by clicking to establish the points and dragging at the same time to produce handles associated with the points. There's no need for great accuracy at this stage.

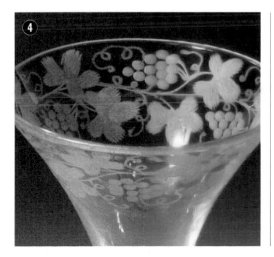

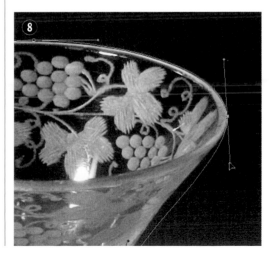

Reduce Noise

Using the Reduce Noise filter continued

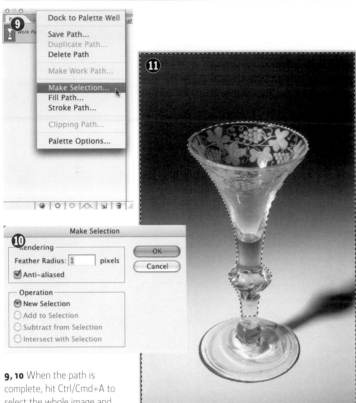

9, 10 When the path is complete, hit Ctrl/Cmd+A to select the whole image and click on the Paths tab where you'll see the path, named as "Work Path." Click on the button at the top right, scroll to Make Selection, and release the mouse. Enter a Feather radius of 1 pixel in the resulting dialog box to soften the edge, and hit OK.

11 Back in the main image window, the glass appears to be excluded from the active background area. The foot of the glass was not included in the path because it's almost free of noise.

12 Run the Reduce Noise filter at the original settings (just hit Ctrl/Cmd+F if you haven't used another filter in the meantime). It's also useful to apply a small amount of Gaussian Blur in an attempt to finally eradicate the background banding.

Using Channels with the Reduce Noise filter

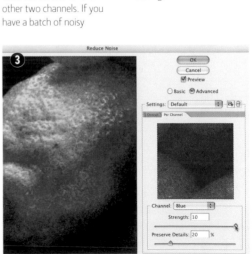

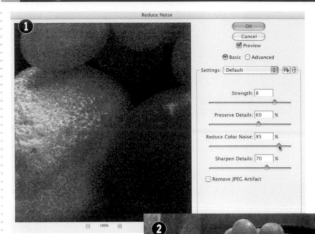

1 The most effective way to track down noise in an RGB image is on a channel-by-channel basis. Normally, the Blue channel will contain the most noise, next the Green, followed by the Red with the least. Reduce Noise allows you to treat them individually by clicking on the Advanced button to reveal the Per Channel tab. The Hand tool allows you to maneuver the image and channel previews separately, so you can view, say, the detailed result on one channel while also being able to see the effect on the overall image. Here, a preliminary setting is made in Basic mode.

2 The picture in question, which would otherwise be consigned to the trash, has elevated noise levels through under-exposure. It was treated with the Auto function in the Curves adjustment to bring the brightness up to an almost acceptable level.

3 Using the Advanced function, go to the Blue channel and set the Strength slider at maximum. A lesser value will suffice for the other two channels. If you have a batch of noisy pictures all shot under similar conditions, it may be worth clicking on the tiny disk icon to save the successful settings for re-use.

Median

This filter is useful in the fight against degraded images. It is used to blend pixels together, thereby reducing image noise. The Median filter works on the brightness of the pixels in an image, replacing those pixels in the search radius whose brightness differs too much from its neighbors with a more average result. It's clear, however, that it is less effective than Dust & Scratches in dealing with random faults, and the result at anything more than a few pixels radius is unacceptably blurred.

How it works

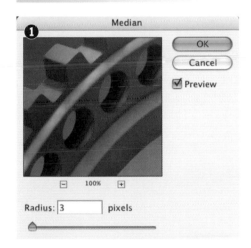

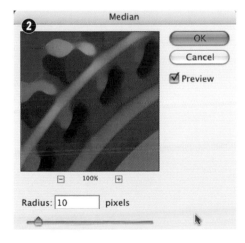

1 Compare this effect, set to a Radius of 3 pixels, with a similar setting in the Dust & Scratches filter. This image has become unacceptably soft in the pursuit of removing faults.

2 Taken to extremes, however, interesting pictorial effects arise. Here the filter is set to a radius of just 10 pixels.

Using the Median filter

If your noise problem is only slight, try this simple maneuver using Median.

1, 2 The original image has noise interference in the dark areas. First, duplicate the layer—drag the layer thumbnail to the "turned page" icon at the foot of the Layers palette, or go to Layer > Duplicate Layer.

3 Open the Median filter and apply it at a 1-pixel radius. You'll rarely need a larger radius unless you are working with very large original images.

4, 5 Change the filtered layer's blending mode to Luminosity. Use the Shift++ (Shift+plus) or Shift+- (Shift+minus) key combinations to cycle through the blending modes.

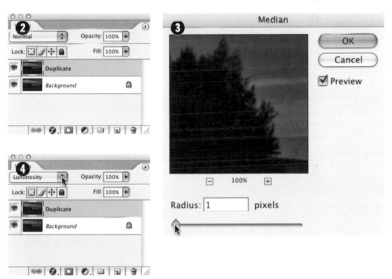

The Pixelate filters

The Pixelate suite harbors some of the most notorious Photoshop filters. As with the Artistic suite, these filters are almost invariably used for effect rather than to improve existing photographs. The filters generally work by breaking the image down into discrete chunks, which are rarely like the pixels you may have encountered before. The shape and make-up of these chunks depends on the filter. Leading the pack is Color Halftone, which separates the channels and converts the square pixels into circles to emulate a halftone screen effect. Crystallize breaks the image into random polygons of a user-specified size. Facet produces a similar, but much more refined, one-shot effect. Fragment sends the image pixels four ways, giving you double double vision. Mezzotint adds various kinds of grain. Mosaic breaks the image into more traditional squares for that old-school pixel look. Finally, Pointillize breaks the image into randomly positioned discs of color.

The Pixelate filters

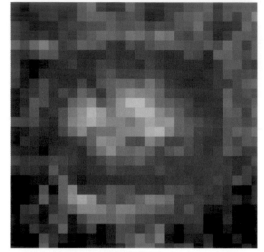

page 103—Mosaic

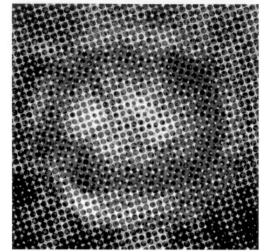

page 104—Color Halftone

page 106—Facet

page 106—Crystallize

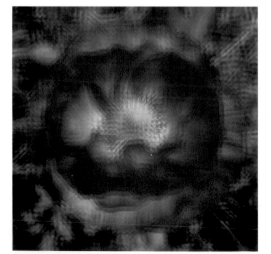

page 107 –Fragment

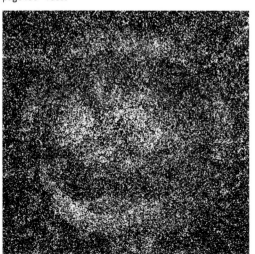

page 108—Mezzotint

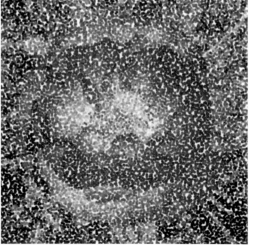

page 112—Pointillize

Mosaic

This filter does not quite live up to its name. For a more realistic mosaic tile effect, you should instead head to the Tiles filter in the Stylize suite (see page 155). The Mosaic filter produces a pixelation effect in which you define the size of the pixels. The dialog box is self-explanatory, with the higher values only of use with very large images.

How it works

1 The example image is treated at a Cell Size of 8...

2 16 ...

3 and 24 pixels.

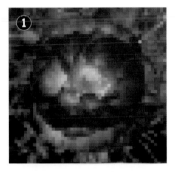

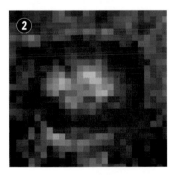

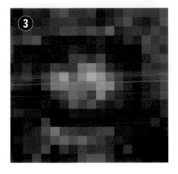

Using the Mosaic filter

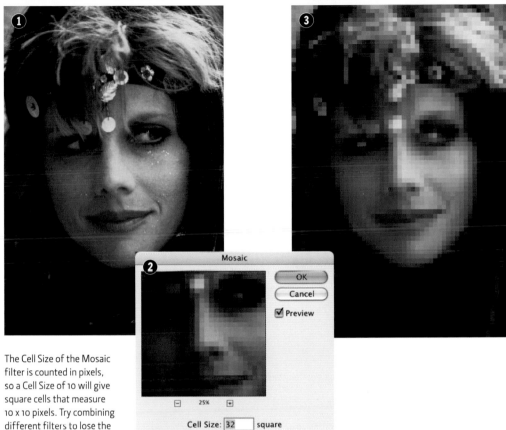

The Cell Size of the Mosaic filter is counted in pixels, so a Cell Size of 10 will give square cells that measure 10 x 10 pixels. Try combining different filters to lose the rigidity of the grid.

1, 2, 3 This image is 1600 pixels wide, and the chosen Cell Size is set at about two percent, or one-fiftieth, of that figure. Your choice of cell size depends on the eventual viewing distance. At a distance, a small cell size can look just like poor definition. Conversely, a large cell size viewed close up will make it hard to see the overall image.

4, 5 Use the Median filter from the Noise suite to soften the mosaic and produce interesting "contour" effects. This example shows the result of applying the filter at a 20-pixel radius.

103

Color Halftone

The printing industry standard for four-color printing (including this book) sets the cyan, magenta, yellow, and black screen angles at 15°, 75°, 0°, and 45° respectively to the vertical. Photoshop perversely measures its screen angles from the horizontal. The default Color Halftone settings are 108°, 162°, 90°, and 45°. A small geometrical calculation (subtracting 90) shows that the Photoshop figures correspond to the printing standard almost exactly, except that cyan is at 18° rather than 15°, and magenta is at 72° rather than 75°. Although the dots produced by Photoshop are colored cyan, magenta, yellow, and black, the filter actually works on the channels in the image. In RGB mode (with only three channels), therefore, the fourth channel in the Color Halftone filter will have no effect. With a grayscale image (where there is only one channel), only the first value in the filter will affect the image. Only a CMYK source image will use all four channels.

How it works

1 The source image here is slightly over 440 pixels wide, so the default radius setting of 8 pixels inevitably gives a very coarse result.

2 Reducing the pixel radius to 4 (the minimum) retains a little more definition.

3 The purer colors of the target image separate out neatly, as well as revealing the underlying screen angles.

4a, 4b Experiment by changing the color mode to CMYK (**Image > Mode > CMYK Color**). At the default setting, the rosette pattern is evident, and magnification to 400% confirms it.

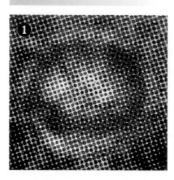

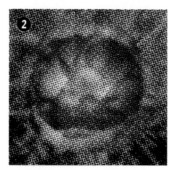

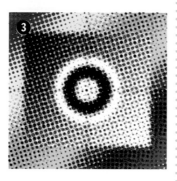

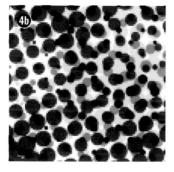

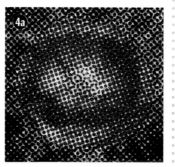

Using the Color Halftone filter

The rosette pattern inherent in the Color Halftone filter can be toned down for a more subtle effect. There are also many possibilities available for blending layers. In this example, the stack is three high, but you can carry on almost ad infinitum. The ceiling in the current version of Photoshop is a generous 8000, but both you and your machine will have expired long before you reach that point.

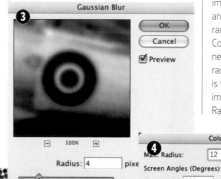

1, 2 Duplicate the image twice in the Layers palette (Ctrl/Cmd+J, Ctrl/Cmd+J), and activate the top layer.

3, 4, 5 Open the Gaussian Blur filter. As a guide, this image is 1860 pixels wide, and the blur is 4 pixels radius. Hit OK and open the Color Halftone filter. You'll need to experiment with the radius figure, but the idea is to leave a recognizable image. Here Maximum Radius has been set to 12.

6 Hide the top layer and activate the middle layer. Go to **Filter** > **Artistic** > **Cutout** and apply the filter at a moderate setting; Number of Levels 5, Edge Simplicity 2, and Edge Fidelity 2.

7, 8 Re-activate the top layer and experiment with its blending mode and opacity relative to the layer/s below. You can cycle through the available blending modes either by clicking on the pop-up menu at the top of the Layers palette or, more easily, by using the key combination Shift++ (Shift+plus) to descend through the alternatives, and Shift+- (Shift+minus) to ascend through them. Set the opacity by typing the first digit of the percentage required—so press 3 for 30% and so on. If you want 33%, type 33 quickly. To quickly return to full opacity, hit 0. The alternative is to use the slider. Here, we've settled on Color at 50% opacity.

9 To alter the image further, try changing the blending mode of the middle layer. Here it's first changed to Hard Mix with opacity reduced to 30%.

10 A more radical effect can then produced by inverting the values in the layer by pressing Ctrl/Cmd+I.

11, 12, 13 Not enough dots? Flatten the image (click on the fly-out button on the Layers palette) and re-apply Color Halftone at the original settings, then go to **Edit** > **Fade Color Halftone** and choose the Difference mode at a low opacity.

Crystallize

Facet

Crystallize averages out adjacent colors and corrals them into solid, vaguely crystalline shapes. It is useful for abstraction, and for effect when combined with blending modes.

How it works

1 Use the solitary slider to select a small Cell Size for a beaten-metal appearance.

2 A large Cell Size (relative to the pixel dimensions of this original) will destroy the image structure completely.

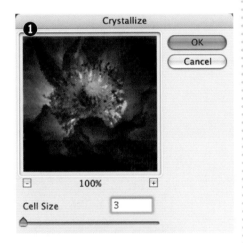

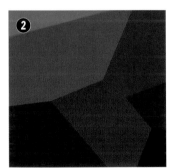

Using the Crystallize filter

Try using this filter on photographs that contain bold colors to achieve striking results.

1, 2, 3 Duplicate the image in the Layers palette. Activate the top layer and open the Crystallize filter. Ignore the zoom feature in the Preview window, as it doesn't work correctly. Set the Cell Size to 50, and click OK.

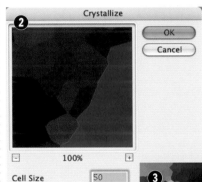

4 Duplicate the filtered layer and change the blending mode of the new layer to Difference. The entire image will turn black.

5 Return to the original filtered layer, invert it (Ctrl/Cmd+I), and set the blending mode to Hard Mix.

Compared with the Crystallize filter, Facet operates only on a small scale. There is no user control, and the effect is probably most useful as a preliminary step in imitating a painterly effect.

How it works

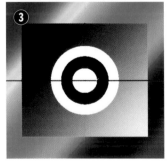

1, 2 The original shows a slight clumping of colors after one application of the filter, but this only becomes apparent when enlarged, as here, to 300%.

3 After 12 applications, the target image loses its fine vertical line, but there is nothing else here for the filter to bite on.

Fragment

Fragment makes four copies of the pixels in an image and offsets them, creating an odd ghosted double-vision effect. Like Facet, it may occasionally be useful for a little light roughing-up of an original prior to a more considered treatment. This is one filter where repeated applications often give a better result than a single one, eventually yielding an interesting crystallized blurring effect.

How it works

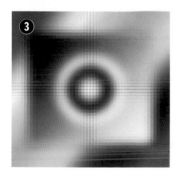

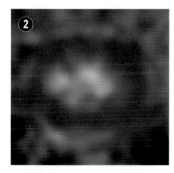

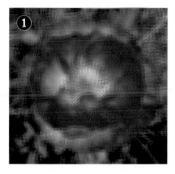

1 With one application, Fragment picks up the image and shakes it a little in its jaws, creating this slightly nausea-inducing effect.

2 After 12 applications, the details of the image have retreated further into the

background, but the crystalline effect is still prominent. In some respects it is similar to the moulded-glass effects of the Glass filter.

3 The target image after the same number of applications is similarly distorted.

Using the Fragment filter

1

2

Try the Fragment filter for a "gauze" effect.

1, 2, 3 What appears to be a simple blur at natural size turns out, at 200% enlargement, to be a rectilinear displacement. Compare the left, unfiltered, side with the treated section.

4 Try adding Diffuse Glow to the initial effect (**Filter > Distort > Diffuse Glow**) with all sliders at mid-way. The effect is reminiscent of early color photography.

107

3

4

Mezzotint

The basis of the artist's mezzotint technique is a metal printing plate that has been treated with a tool designed to produce a fine mesh of pinpricks that will retain ink. Without further treatment, the inked-up plate would print almost solid black, albeit with a pattern of the ink-retaining pinpricks. To make an image, a scraper is used to remove ink from the areas of the plate that are required to appear white in the final print. Intermediate (gray) areas are only lightly scraped. The Photoshop filter struggles to produce a similar effect; instead it often results in overly strong black patterns masking the image below. There are three sets of patterns—dots, lines, and strokes, which, combined, offer a total of ten effects.

How it works

1 When the filter is applied without further treatment, the result is somewhat uninteresting, as illustrated here with Fine Dots applied.

2 To modify this effect, go immediately to **Edit > Fade Mezzotint**, and select Soft Light as the blending mode to achieve a less violent effect.

Other blending modes, such as Overlay or Screen, may be just as effective in individual cases, but the remaining nine mezzotint patterns are shown here with Soft Light employed as the fade option.

3 Medium Dots.

4 Long Lines.

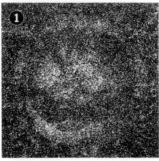

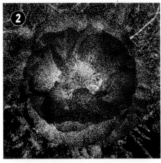

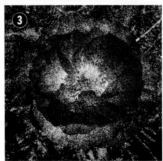

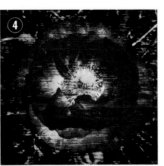
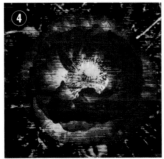

Using the Mezzotint filter

Selective masking can help to moderate the effect of the Mezzotint filter.

1, 2 Duplicate the source image (Ctrl/Cmd+J). To make it easier to create a selection, click and drag on the bottom right corner of the image window to reveal the gray work area. Next, use the Lasso tool to select the "land" part of the picture.

3, 4 Click on the Add Layer Mask icon at the foot of the Layers palette. A new thumbnail appears alongside the image thumbnail, with a miniature representation of the land area in white and a chain icon between the two. The frame around the image thumbnail has also moved to the mask thumbnail to show that it's active—you can re-activate the latter by clicking on it at any time.

5, 6 You can get an idea of what's happening by clicking on the Channels tab and making the newly-created "Layer 1 Mask" visible. Returning to the normal view, a pink veil has appeared over the masked area. In this way you can choose whether or not to have the mask visible while working. Visible or not, it will be active as long as the chain link icon is present.

7 Click on the image thumbnail (the pink mask will disappear for the moment), and select the magic Wand tool. Our intention here is to select the bridge handrail where it is silhouetted against the sky. There are a number of different colors present in this area, so set the wand tolerance at about 30 pixels, and uncheck the contiguous function. The first selection will inevitably not include all of the desired areas, so capture them by clicking on the elusive parts while holding down the Shift key. Ignore other areas captured, such as the grass, as they are not significant in the selection.

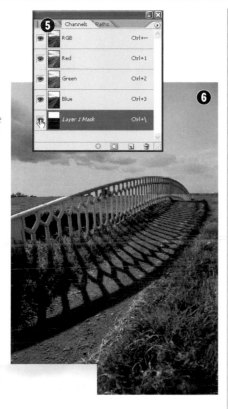

❺

❻

❼

8,9 Click once more on the mask thumbnail and hit Delete. Now, if you return to the Channels palette and hide the main image to show just the mask channel, you'll see that the handrail has been subtracted from the sky area. Additionally, the clump of trees at the extreme left has also been removed.

❽

❾

10 Return to the Layers palette and click on the image thumbnail. There are a number of options to "improve" the lackluster sky. In this case, direct action means importing a completely new one. Open a suitable sky image—ideally one of a width and resolution similar to the

❿

12 The two elements are now in place, and they can be treated separately with different Mezzotint filters.

13 As a start, treat the sky with Long Strokes, then use **Edit > Fade Long Strokes** to reduce it to 80% opacity.

⑫

⑬

14 Activate the masked landscape by clicking on the image—not the mask—thumbnail, and try a different Mezzotint. This is the result of applying Medium Dots, and then fading the effect to 80% opacity with Linear Dodge as the blending mode.

landscape image, although the rough quality of the Mezzotint filter will compensate for a less-than perfect match. Drag the layer thumbnail into the main image window of the target document. A black line will surround the window as soon as the imported layer has safely arrived.

⑪

11 The imported image shows up as a new layer. Use the Move tool (key V) to shift the sky around until it fits. You may also have to resize it (Use Ctrl/Cmd+T to bring up the Transform tool). Reduce the layer opacity temporarily to check its size and position relative to the landscape, then drag the layer downward in the Layers palette so that it sits above the background (the original untouched image).

⑭

Pointillize

Though we're still waiting for a Jackson Pollock-style paint-spatter filter, the speed-Seurat Pointillize filter has been in the Photoshop armory since the dawn of time. It works by reducing the image to dots of a specified size (between 3 and 300 pixels), randomly offsetting them, and filling the resulting space with the currently selected background color. The filter is most effective at low values, with high values resembling the molecular models beloved by chemistry teachers.

How it works

1 With a Cell Size of 3, the dots are almost a little too small, and your eye is drawn toward the background color more than the dots that make up the image.

2 Increasing the Cell Size to 5 creates more recognizable dots, and gives a more stylized result.

3 For variety, click in the background color box in the Tools palette and select a pale yellow. The background tint changes accordingly when the filter is re-applied.

4 The target image clearly shows how the filter distributes colors either side of the underlying color.

5 This target in grayscale mode shows that there are also possibilities for applying the Pointillize filter to monochrome subjects.

6 Returning to color mode, a close-up of the filter's effect (using the default black and white color palette) applied to a plain gray image reveals the dot structure and color range that's produced.

The Pointillize filter needs a helping hand to produce a realistic "painted" effect. But even with these extra moves, we are still some way from achieving a convincing artistic reproduction.

1, 2 To get some texture into the surface, first select all (Ctrl/Cmd+A). Move to the Channels palette, and create a new channel by clicking on the turned-page icon at the foot of the palette. Paste (Ctrl/Cmd+V) the copied image into the new channel.

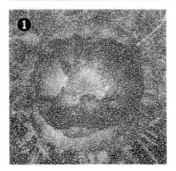

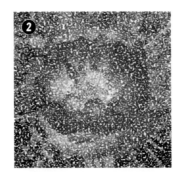

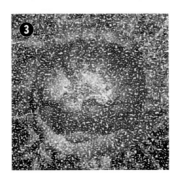

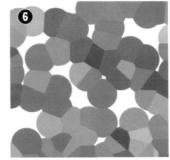

3, 4, 5 Apply the Pointillize filter to the grayscale channel. The choice of Cell Size here is largely trial and error, since the Preview window is not entirely helpful with this filter. As a guide, if you can still see the main structure of the image but the detail is suppressed, then you're in range. In any case, make a note of the cell size that you choose. I found Cell Size 8 to be about right. Use the **Edit > Fade** function immediately to change the filter's blending mode to Overlay, but retain 100% opacity. Finally, apply Gaussian Blur at a 3 pixel radius.

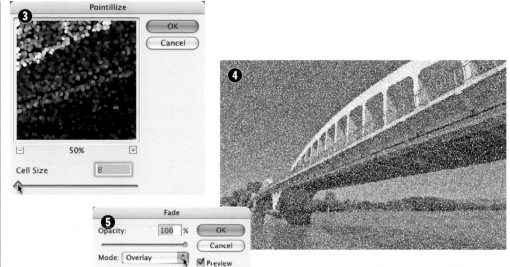

6, 7 Return to the Layers palette and duplicate the image twice (Ctrl/Cmd+J). Hide the top layer, activate the middle layer, and go to **Filter > Render > Lighting Effects**. Change the default settings to a Directional Light Type, and set the Texture Channel to Alpha 1 (the channel that you just created). Uncheck White is high. Hit OK. The result will look overly strong, but we'll tone it down later.

8 Activate the top layer and apply the Pointillize filter at the original settings. (Don't just hit Ctrl/Cmd+F, or you'll get a second application of Lighting Effects.)

9, 10 Now adjust the blending modes of the top two layers. You can cycle down and up through the alternatives by keying Shift++ (Shift+plus) and Shift+- (Shift+minus). Here the top layer is set to Hard Light at 70%, and the middle layer left at Normal but with only 50% opacity.

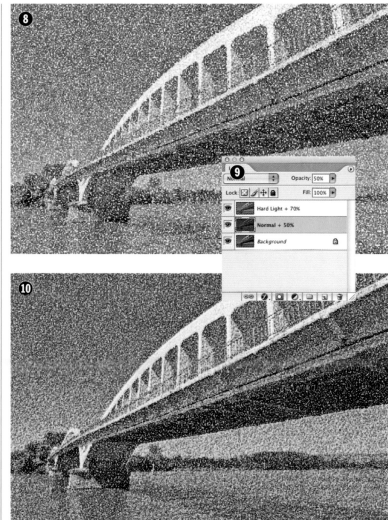

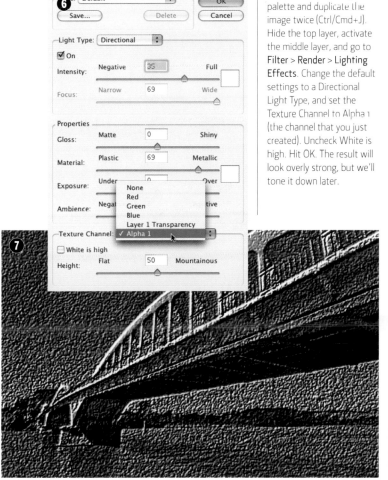

The Render filters

The Render suite is a curious mixture. Clouds and Difference Clouds are used for far more than just making clouds. The former is often employed to add "natural" variance to flat areas; the latter is best used in the preparation of unusual backgrounds. Fibers, a recent introduction, is a good standby for a kind of vertical noise at very low and faded settings. Equal restraint is necessary with Lens Flare. Its glossy, over-lit atmosphere, with accompanying iris shapes, is a well-worn Photoshop cliché. Finally, there is the complex and very useful Lighting Effects filter, almost an application in its own right. For the Photoshop novice, it's also a good primer for the even more complex layer styles and effects that the application offers.

The Render filters

page 113—Fibers

page 114—Clouds

page 116—Difference Clouds

page 117—Lens Flare

page 118—Lighting Effects

Fibers

The Fibers filter works by taking the foreground and background colors and using them to produce a random pattern. The Variance slider controls the contrast and spread of each color, and the Strength slider the amount of striation—with high values giving long, drawn-out fibers. It is useful as an alternative to the Noise filter—use at higher values and fade the result. Strangely, unlike the Clouds pattern, which is randomly regenerated every time you hit Ctrl/Cmd+F to rerun the filter, Fibers will repeat the filter with exactly the same pattern. To regenerate the Fibers pattern, you must use the Randomize button.

How it works

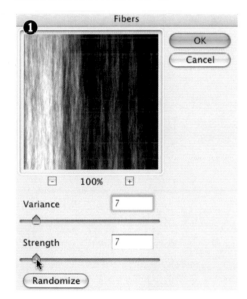

1 A typically furry first effort.

2 Fibers usually requires an additional fading stage. It responds to changes in the color palette in the same way as Clouds (see page 114).

Using the Fibers filter

The Fibers filter is best employed in a two-stage process, as a screen overlay on the image to be treated.

1, 2 Reset the color palette to black and white (key D). Add a blank layer to the existing image, and fill it with black or white (the Fibers filter will not operate on an empty layer). Apply Fibers at maximum strength.

3 Change the blending mode of the filtered layer to Soft Light and reduce the opacity of it to 50%.

4 The close-up view reveals the effect of the Fibers filter on this image.

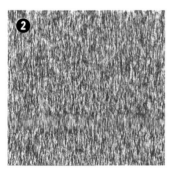

Clouds

The Clouds filter works with the current foreground and background colors to produce a soft, mottled texture. Holding down the Alt/Option key when you select the filter will produce a harder, higher contrast version of the effect. The filter is a useful standby when manipulating images that need variation in large flat areas of color. It is also very helpful in disguising the artificial look of pictures that are made up of several component layers.

How it works

1 With the color palette set to the default black and white, the result will resemble this image.

2 If you then fade the filter using the Soft Light blending mode (**Edit > Fade Clouds > Soft Light**), the original image will receive a light and variable cloudy treatment.

3 Changing the foreground color to a bright red will give a different result.

4 Changing the background color, this time to a bright yellow, will give yet another clouds variant.

5 Here, we've applied the Clouds filter to the sky area only. A dark blue and a white were sampled from the existing sky for the foreground and background colors, and the result was immediately faded using the Pin Light blending mode. Although the filter gives realistic cloud shapes, it's difficult to reproduce the density and texture of the true clouds that can be seen on the right-hand side of the image.

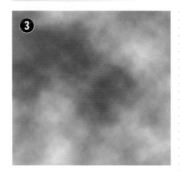

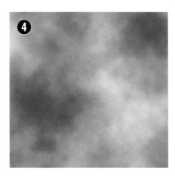

Using the Clouds filter

If your studio space doesn't allow for large backgrounds to shoot against, try creating virtual versions using Clouds filter. You can then use the Extract filter (see page 178) to place your subject in front of them.

1 Make a new RGB document 2400 pixels wide and 3600 pixels high—the same ratio as the 35mm camera format. Set the color palette in the toolbox with two complementary colors.

2, 3 Apply the Clouds filter and then the Polar Coordinates filter from the Distort suite (see page 84). Choose Polar to Rectangular for this result.

4, 5 Alternatively, use Clouds exactly as above, but use the Glowing Edges filter from the Stylize suite, at full strength, instead of Polar Coordinates. The Glowing Edges filter creates a background image that resembles a closeup of strands of woolen yarn.

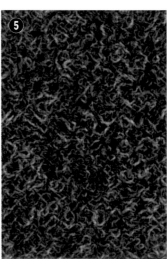

Creating water with the Clouds filter

If you are looking for an image of rippled water, this technique offers a good simulation.

1 Make a new, very tall document, and call it "sea." This one is 1200 pixels wide and 5000 pixels high. The usable image width at the end of this process will be under half this width, so it's a good idea to over- rather than under-estimate your size requirement.

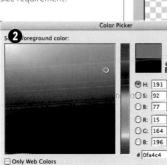

2 Hit the D key to reset the color palette to black and white. Click in the black area to access the color picker. Choose a suitably watery, medium-toned color. Repeat the operation with the white (background color) panel, but choose a lighter tint.

3 The two new colors are now installed in the palette.

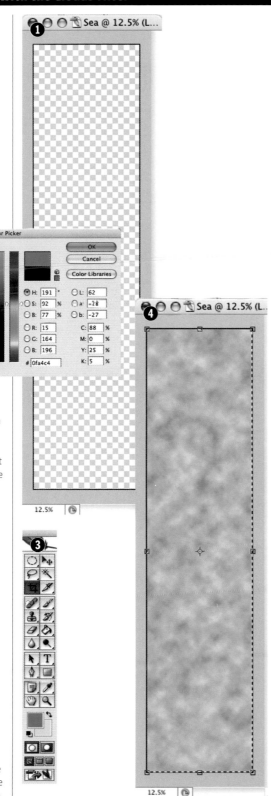

4 Apply the Clouds filter, select all (Ctrl/Cmd+A), and then Ctrl/Cmd+T to transform the image.

5 Click on the top-center handle and drag it down almost the full depth of the window. Hit OK and, with the selection still active, go to **Image > Crop**.

6, 7 Keep the selection active, choose **Edit > Transform > Perspective**, and drag the top-left handle toward the center line of the image. Hit OK when you see

the desired amount of distortion, then deselect (Ctrl/Cmd+D). You may find it easier to increase the window size and zoom in to see what you're doing. Use the Crop tool (key C) to trim off the unusable areas.

8, 9, 10 Compare the result with a couple of variations. The second version was treated with Paint Daubs while still at the larger size. The third version, with the same color palette, used repeated applications of Difference Clouds.

TIP

To increase the effect of this filter, hold down the Alt/Option and Ctrl/Cmd keys when selecting it. The same applies to Difference Clouds (see page 116).

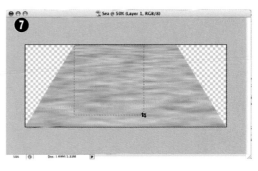

Difference Clouds

Equipped with the same pattern generator as Clouds, Difference Clouds works directly on the underlying image rather than simply replacing it. As its name suggests, the filter uses the same algorithm as the Difference blending mode to produce the final image. Indeed, this filter produces exactly the same effects as running the default Clouds filter, then immediately following it with Edit > Fade Clouds and selecting the Difference blending mode.

How it works

1 The default color palette setting gives a curious "solarized" result.

2 Canceling and re-applying the filter confirms that there is a "random generator" at work, since the effect is quite different.

3 The target image shows the difference when the filter runs over color and grayscale areas.

4, 5 As with the Clouds filter, changing the foreground and background palette colors will give different results.

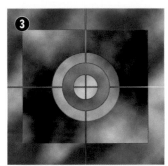

Using the Difference Clouds filter

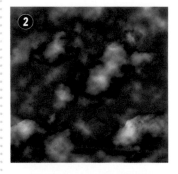

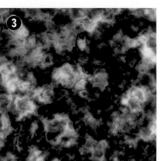

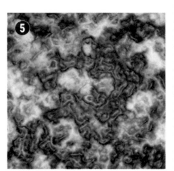

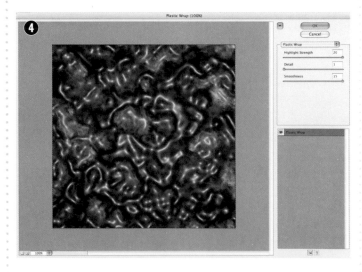

Like Clouds, the Difference Clouds filter can be used for more than just creating skies. Here, we've used its random properties to make a texture similar to abalone.

1, 2 Find an existing cloudscape and apply Difference Clouds.

3 Repeat the filter multiple times to build up a complex pattern. This example has been filtered 12 times.

4, 5 Select the Plastic Wrap filter in the Artistic suite, apply it, and immediately fade it to 50% with the Screen blending mode.

Lens Flare

This filter produces the archetypal, and some might say clichéd, lens flare. There are four choices of lens simulation in the Lens Flare panel, as well as the option to choose the exact position of the sun in your picture. It goes almost without saying that the position of the flare should tend to match the lighting plot in the original picture, and that, in this case, less is definitely more.

How it works

1 Running the filter on a plain black ground reveals the underlying image used by the zoom lens setting.

2 At the 50–300mm zoom setting, the characteristic flare circles appear diagonally across the frame.

3 Single flares occur with the 35mm ...

4 ... 105mm ...

5 ... and movie settings.

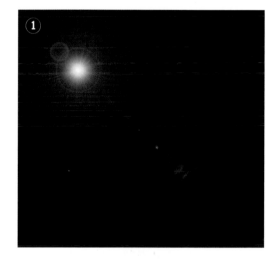

Using the Lens Flare filter

Like Fibers, Lens Flare is best applied to a separate layer and then blended with the subject.

1 Shot on a bright but overcast day, this picture is an ideal candidate for enhancement. To get maximum flexibility with the Lens Flare filter, increase the Canvas Size by about 150% in both axes. Make a new layer and fill it with black.

2 Open the filter and position the flare by clicking and dragging. You can't see the underlying picture, but it's not important at this stage. Just make sure the trail of smaller ghost images is below the main flare.

3, 4 Change the black layer's blending mode to Screen. This will reveal the underlying image again, so you can now position the flare accurately. You can also rotate or resize the flare layer using Ctrl/Cmd+T.

5 You can take further advantage of the additional canvas area by treating the base image again with Lens Flare. Position the flare center in the blank, extra canvas, and choose Lens Type 35mm to achieve a simple haze with just a few iris artifacts. All that's left is to crop the image to its original format.

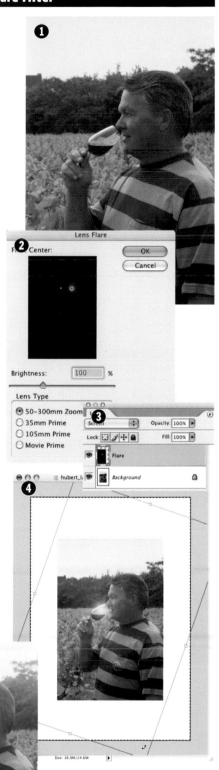

RENDER
Lighting Effects

The Lighting Effects filter is a powerful and complex thing, and whole books have been written on the intricacies of its use. Essentially, it emulates the effect of a new light source in your image by brightening certain areas and darkening others. Its effect can be enhanced with the addition of a displacement map, giving a more realistic 3D appearance to the way the light falls.

How it works

1 The default settings produce a gentle effect with light spilling upward from the lower right corner.

2 Click on the Style pop-up to access the built-in presets. Choose 2 O'clock Spotlight to get an idea of how the system works. Almost every setting in the main panel changes automatically. In the preview window (make sure you check Preview) the light's direction, central point, and area of illumination have been reset. Other changes appear on the right side of the window: the spotlight's color has changed to pale yellow, the subject's own reflective qualities and body color are modified in the Properties section below; and only the Texture Channel (of which more later) remains untouched for now.

3 The result is, however, uninspiring, but you can use these settings as a starting-point for improvement.

4 The tiny handles in the preview window can be clicked and dragged to make changes in the spotlight's properties.

5 The remaining settings are also easily changed. Here the spotlight's

Intensity, Focus, and Color have been altered, while the subject has been given a more shiny and metallic look. The image has also been brightened by slight over-exposure and an increase in the amount of ambient light (in other words, the background light that's not coming from the spotlight). In addition, the subject's own color has been further amended.

6 The result of all of this activity is considerably more dramatic.

7 If you are not content with just one light, return to the preview window to add another by clicking on the light bulb button. The cursor changes to a light bulb that can be dragged to the desired position in the window, and then modified as per the original light. Bear in mind that there must always be one light active in the window. These modified settings can be retained for re-use, if desired, by clicking on Save near the top of the panel. They will then take their place in the pop-up list of Styles.

8 New lights always appear as spotlights in the preview window, but they

can be easily changed to Omni(directional) or Directional in the Light Type dialog near the top of the panel. Here are three Omni lights with the background darkened for clarity.

9 For practical purposes, and especially for achieving 3D effects, the directional light is the most useful. In this

simple example, a directional light is positioned at the top left in the preview window, with Red (the already existing channel which, along with the Green and Blue channels, form the target RGB image) selected as the Texture Channel, to achieve a slightly three-dimensional appearance.

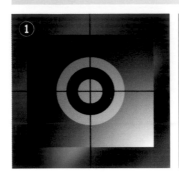

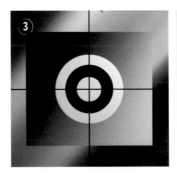

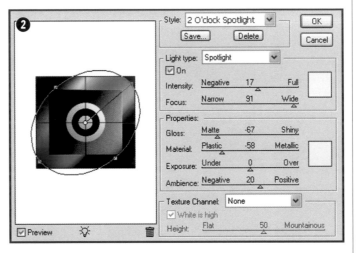

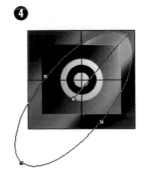

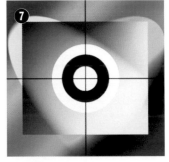

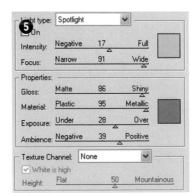

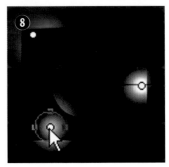

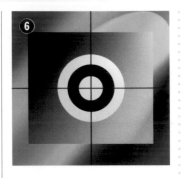

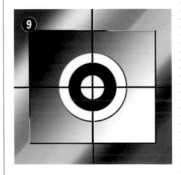

One of the most powerful feature of the Lighting Effects filter is the Texture Channel. This technique uses an indirect method to finely control the result.

1 As shot, this image is a reasonably true representation of a two-thousand-year-old Roman mosaic floor, but a thin layer of dust, combined with flat interior lighting, is making it difficult to see the original glass tesserae.

2 First, select all (Ctrl/Cmd+A) and copy the image. Go to the Channels palette, click on the turned page icon to create a new channel, and paste the copy into it. Return to the Layers palette.

3 Make a new blank layer, go to **Edit > Fill**, and choose 50% Gray as the fill. Click OK to apply the fill. Open the Lighting Effects filter, select Directional as the Light Type, and Alpha 1 (the new channel that we created) as the Texture Channel. In additional, check White is High, and adjust the Intensity slider so that the preview window shows a mid-gray image. You may also need to adjust the direction of the light in the small preview window to make the image visible. Hit OK.

4 The filtered result has darker values in the shadow areas. You may need a couple of attempts at changing the Intensity before you achieve the desired result.

5, 6 Change the filtered layer's blending mode to Color Burn and reduce its opacity to 50%.

7 For a more emphatic, though rather artificial, effect, select the background layer and run **Image > Adjustments > Auto Color**.

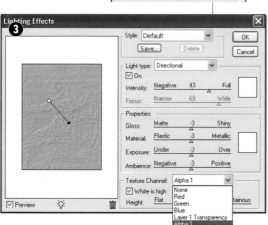

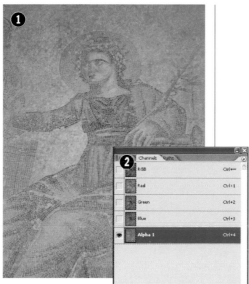

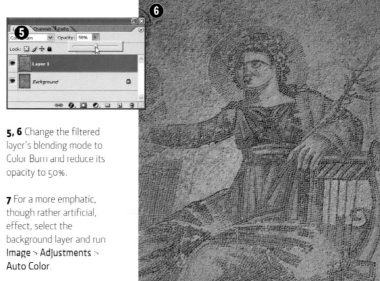

The Sharpen filters

Take a look in your photographic trash can. Among the pictures you discard, what's the most common fault? A small bet says that it's lack of sharpness. Photoshop's own Sharpen suite has been augmented by many third-party filters and plug-ins, but there are still useful features here, of which the best are Smart Sharpen (new in CS2) and Unsharp Mask. The other three are devoid of controls, so are really only useful for a quick and dirty fix. And by the way, how sharp is sharp enough? A can of beans on a freeway billboard may have dots the size of your fist, but distance and your (very moderate) speed of passing lend apparent sharpness. The original was most likely shot on a large-format studio film camera, or a twenty-thousand-dollar digital back which captures 22 million pixels. The screen image appearing on the back of a regular digital camera boasts only around 120,000 pixels but looks absolutely pin-sharp, bright, and perfect. It's worth bearing in mind the target audience of your image before subjecting it to unnecessary sharpening.

120

The Sharpen filters

page 121—Sharpen

page 121—Sharpen More

page 123—Sharpen Edges

page 124—Smart Sharpen

page 126—Unsharp Mask

Sharpen and Sharpen More

The basic effect of the Sharpen filter is to increase the contrast between pixels in an image. Without any control over the strength of the filter, though, it often leads to ugly, bright artifacts appearing on the image. The Sharpen More filter operates in exactly the same way as Sharpen, but at double strength.

How it works

1 After one application of Sharpen, the full-size image shows no perceptible change at this enlargement.

2, 3 At 300% enlargement, compare the untreated image with the result of one application...

4 ...and four applications.

5 Now, the full-size version shows a clear difference, but at the expense of increased pixelation and incipient color

edge effects. Note that the rearmost petals appear to have sharpened considerably, but the foremost parts are beyond repair.

6, 7 A closeup of the target image after five applications of the Sharpen and Sharpen More filters respectively. Notice the color that has been introduced into the gray areas of the image.

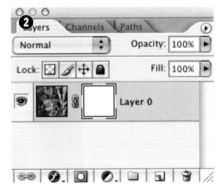

There is already a striking difference between the foreground and background in this image, but a little careful sharpening will heighten the effect.

1 Double-click on the Background layer thumbnail and hit OK when the dialog appears. This unlocks the layer and enables the creation of a layer mask.

2 Go to Layer > Layer Mask > Reveal All, and a new thumbnail appears alongside the existing one, together with a link icon.

Sharpen and Sharpen More

3 Select the Eraser tool (key E) and, in Brush mode with the opacity set to 100%, erase the blurred background. Use the "[" and "]" keys to quickly change the size of your brush. Before you start, make sure that the mask thumbnail is active—shown by the heavier frame surrounding it. Continue until all of the background has been removed.

4, 5 Click on the original image thumbnail to activate it (a vital step, otherwise you'll be sharpening the mask instead of the image), and apply the Sharpen filter two or three times. Go to **Layer > Disable Layer Mask** and you'll see the original blurred background reappear.

6 To make a greater contrast between the sharp and blurred areas, you can re-use the layer mask. Return to the Layer menu, enable the mask once more, and use the shortcut Ctrl/Cmd+I to invert it. The background reappears minus the subject. Click on the image thumbnail and go to **Filter > Blur > Blur More**. Apply this filter three or four times.

7, 8 Disable the layer mask once more to see the final result. Comparing the original with the treated version, it's clear that the Sharpen filter can be effective in moderation.

9, 10, 11 Choosing Unsharp Mask rather than Sharpen gives a quite different result.

12, 13 The more flexible approach of the Smart Sharpen filter (see page 124) enables closer control of highlights and shadows.

122

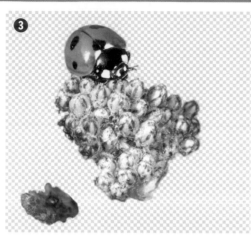

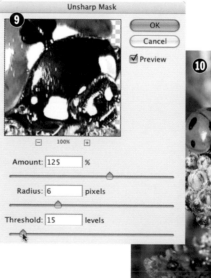

Sharpen Edges

The logic of this filter, and of its more sophisticated companions Smart Sharpen and Unsharp Mask, is that the perception of lack of sharpness is concentrated along distinct edges in the image, so that is where the useful effort should go. Conversely, the flat areas should be left alone to avoid introducing unnecessary artifacts.

How it works

1 After one application, the difference between this effect and the previous one with the plain Sharpen filter is clear where the petal is seen against a dark ground, as this is where the maximum sharpening is concentrated.

2 Running the filter again, a stronger effect is seen.

3 With four applications, there is serious degradation in closeup.

4 However, the full-size version of the image still seems acceptable.

Smart Sharpen

When you have a particularly explicit kind of blur to eradicate, choose Smart Sharpen. It offers a choice of Basic or Advanced working mode. For flexibility, always choose Advanced for its ability to adjust shadows and highlights separately. It's also a good idea to accept the slower response of More Accurate. Smart Sharpen inherits the Amount and Radius controls from Unsharp Mask, but adds a choice of three Blur settings specific to the type of blur to be remedied. In Advanced mode, there are two further tabs: Shadow and Highlight, with identical controls.

How it works

1a, 1b At the default settings in Basic mode, there is reasonable sharpening and slight fringing, seen more easily in close up.

2 After increasing the Radius to 1.5 pixels, compare the effects of the three Remove settings: Gaussian Blur...

3 ... Lens Blur ...

4 ... and Motion Blur.

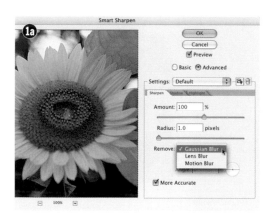

Smart Sharpen Demo

The in-focus areas of this image need further sharpening, but without adding "sharpen artifacts" to the out-of-focus areas. A mask would be difficult to create here, but Smart Sharpen can help.

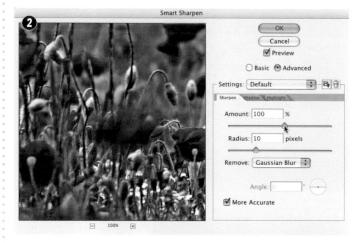

1, 2, 3 Using just the basic controls at moderate settings, there's a considerable change in the central area of the image, but the edge effects associated with the highlights are looking over-emphasized.

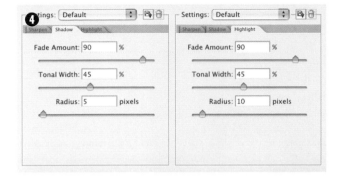

7, 8, 9 Using the exact same settings on an original image with many dark areas shows quite a different reaction to the filter. The subject jumps out with excessive contrast throughout, and it is best tamed by changing its blending mode—here Luminosity has been used.

10 The Remove settings at the base of the Basic tab can have a radical effect on the filtered result. In this case, Motion Blur was selected (though there's plainly no motion blur in the original subject)—compare this unfaded result with the effect produced in the first attempt, using Gaussian Blur removal.

4, 5, 6 Switching to the Advanced tabs, try setting the separate Shadow and Highlight sliders to identical values. The edge effects have now calmed down and look more realistic.

Unsharp Mask

There is no actual mask involved with this filter, unsharp or otherwise. The name refers back to a pre-digital-era platemaking technique of sandwiching a thin and slightly blurred negative version of the original image to the original film positive to make an edge mask. The intent, then as now, was to increase edge sharpness. With the Photoshop version, however, the Threshold control allows one to choose whether to employ sharpening solely to the edges or across the entire image.

How it works

1 The Unsharp Mask filter includes three sliders: Amount runs up to 500% on an exponential scale, but normal use will be under 200%; Radius determines the number of adjacent pixels which will enter into the sharpness calculation; and Threshold looks at the brightness difference of neighboring pixels—the lowest setting will sharpen all pixels, while a setting of 10, for example, will sharpen only those pixels whose brightness differs from their neighbors by 10 or more.

2 One application at: Amount 175%, Radius 1, Threshold 0, has an apparently beneficial effect.

3 At 300% enlargement, however, you can see aggressive noise and the beginnings of color fringing at the petal edges.

4 Starting over and increasing the Threshold level to 20 eradicates most of the noise and color fringing.

5 Doubling the radius setting to 2 and raising the threshold to 100, however, brings no further gains.

Using the Unsharp Mask filter

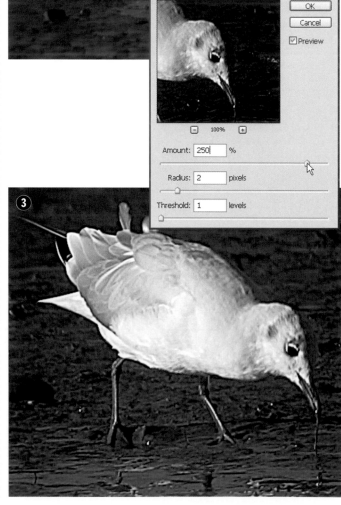

The standard approach to sharpening applies the effect equally to all three channels in an RGB document. The Blue channel, however, is often home to more than its fair share of irritating noise, so sharpening Blue can simply lead to sharper noise in your image.

1, 2, 3 For ease of comparison, first duplicate the background layer and sharpen it in the conventional way, so that all channels are equally affected by Unsharp Mask.

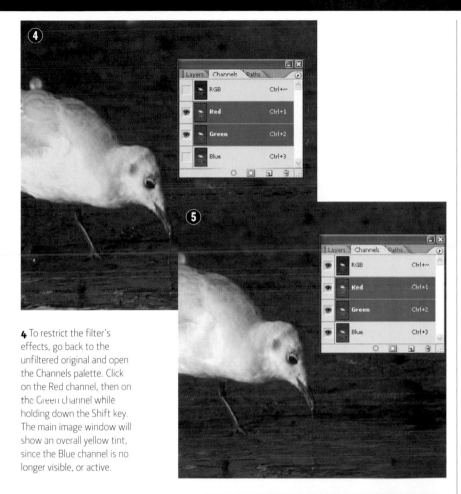

4 To restrict the filter's effects, go back to the unfiltered original and open the Channels palette. Click on the Red channel, then on the Green channel while holding down the Shift key. The main image window will show an overall yellow tint, since the Blue channel is no longer visible, or active.

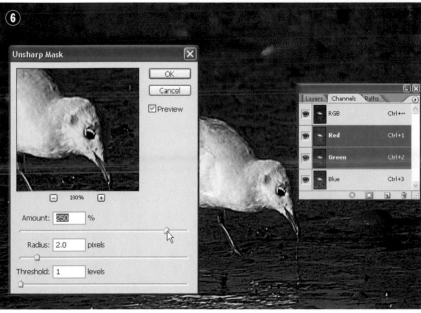

Unsharp Mask

Amount: 250 %

Radius: 2.0 pixels

Threshold: 1 levels

5 Next, click on the square to the left of the RGB thumbnail. This makes all channels visible, but only Red and Green are active.

6 Open the Unsharp Mask filter, and apply it at the original settings. Although the panel's preview window shows the yellow tint on the bird, you can see the effect in full color in the main image window.

7, 8 Compare the unfiltered Blue channel with the filtered version from the first example ...

9, 10 ... with the matching full-color results.

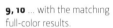

The Sketch filters

The distinction between the Sketch suite and its companions in the Artistic suite is obscure. In general, Sketch filters use the foreground and background colors to produce marks or strokes. If those colors are black and white, you'll most likely see a grayscale result. Just as in the Artistic suite, there are heroes, villains, and interlopers here. All of the filters in this suite take a bit of work to combine them effectively with a photographic source.

page 130—Bas Relief

page 132—Chalk & Charcoal

page 134—Charcoal

page 136—Chrome

page 129—Conté Crayon

page 135—Graphic Pen

page 138—Halftone Pattern

page 140—Note Paper

page 141—Photocopy

page 142—Plaster

page 144—Reticulation

page 145—Stamp

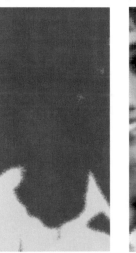
page 146—Torn Edges

page 147—Water Paper

128

Conté Crayon

Real conté crayons were invented in France in the 1790s to compensate for a shortage of English graphite. The new formulation substituted clay for a large proportion of the original graphite. The Photoshop version of this tool produces an effect similar to that of the Rough Pastels filter (see page 32). The big difference is that Rough Pastels keeps the colors of the original image, while this filter replaces them with the foreground and background colors. The controls are almost identical, but there is also a subtle difference in the stroke quality. Conté Crayon's stroke has no directional emphasis—the effect is curiously more rubbed than drawn.

How it works

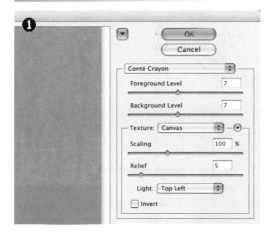

1, 2 With five sliders, two pop-ups, and a checkbox, you need a strategy to manage this filter. First, centralize the foreground and background sliders, leaving Canvas as the default texture with scaling at 100%, a low value for Relief, Light Direction at Top Left, and Invert unchecked.

3 Increase the Foreground and Background levels to near-maximum to increase the spread of texture.

4 You can increase the scale of the texture by up to 200%. Here, the maximum value has been used with the Sandstone texture.

5 A more subtle effect is produced by manipulating the foreground and background levels.

Using the Conté Crayon filter

Beside the built-in textures in Conté Crayon, you can use any suitable image file to create a surface texture to work on.

1 Although this image of a crop being harvested already contains some texture in the shape of the field and the grooves cut by the combine harvester, the overall tone of the image makes it feel very flat. We can easily change this with the help of the Conté Crayon filter.

2 If you have already installed the "Goodies" from the "Resources and Extras" disc that comes with Photoshop, then you can find some additional high-resolution textures. Open the Conté Crayon filter and click on the small arrow next to the Texture menu to reveal the Load Texture command. This will bring up a file browser, from which you can navigate to the Goodies > Photoshop CS2 > Textures for Lighting Effects folder.

3 The texture that we've selected is Frozen Rain, set at Foreground Level 11, Background Level 7, Scaling 100%, Relief 5, Light coming from the top-left, and the original color palette set to the default black and white. The result is the texture that we're after, but the filter has replaced all of the color in the image with gray.

4 This can be remedied by going to **Edit > Fade Conté Crayon**, fading its opacity to 20%, and setting the blending mode to Linear Light. The result has more interesting tonal variations across the entire image.

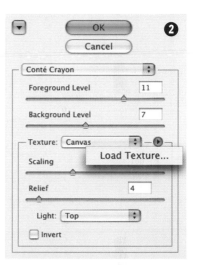

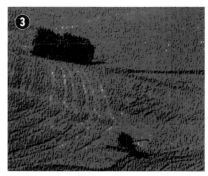

129

SKETCH Bas Relief

The Bas Relief filter produces a 3D, sculpted result by reducing the image to the foreground and background colors, using, by default, the foreground to replace dark areas of the image, and the background to replace the light areas. Altering the Light direction can change this. The best results usually come with the Detail slider kept high and the Smoothness slider kept low. Most other combinations result in an overly blurred image. Try using it in conjunction with Edit > Fade, or to generate textures, as shown in the following examples.

How it works

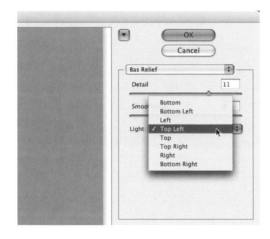

1 Here, the Bas Relief filter has been applied with Detail set to 11, Smoothness 4, and Light coming from the top left. It gives a traditional 3D gloss to the image.

2 With Bottom Right Light selected, the image appears to be impressed into the surface rather than raised.

3 With the light direction restored to Top Right and both sliders at minimum value, a curious contour map effect appears.

4 Raise the Detail slider to maximum and leave the Smoothness at level 1 for a flatter, but much more pitted effect.

5 Try changing the color palette before applying the filter to achieve this nearly gold-foil appearance.

6, 7 The target image (with default color palette restored) clearly demonstrates the offsetting effect on fine lines and strong contrast edges.

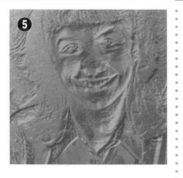

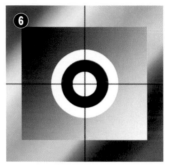

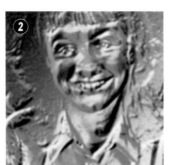

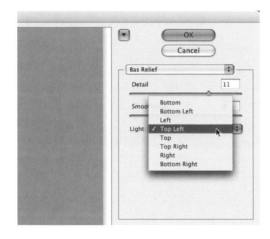

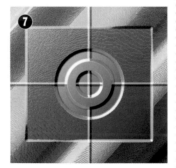

Using the Bas Relief filter

The effect of Bas Relief on its own is almost always too strong. Edit > Fade is the obvious strategy, but it involves a lot of speculative clicking until the right solution is found. Try layer blending modes instead.

1 This flatly-lit landscape could use a little more grit. First, duplicate the existing layer (Ctrl/Cmd+J). Apply the filter to the duplicate layer at a high Detail value (14) and low Smoothness (3).

2, 3 The result is gray and almost incomprehensible, but don't go to **Edit > Fade** to save the day—just cycle through the layer blending modes by hitting Shift++ (Shift+plus) or Shift+- (Shift+minus). We've settled on Overlay in this example. You can also vary the upper layer's opacity by keying in a numeral—for example, 8 represents 80%. Press 0 to return to 100%.

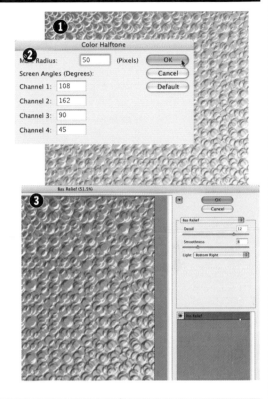

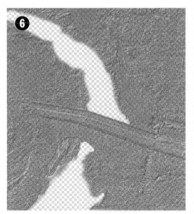

4 This combination of blend (Overlay) and opacity gives a reasonable result.

5, 6, 7 If you prefer no grit in your water, just use the Eraser set to minimum hardness and erase the river area. Viewed by itself, the filtered layer shows the absent watercourse—there's no need for great accuracy in erasing except around the bridge parapet.

Creating texture with the Bas Relief filter

To create your own unique backgrounds or texture files for use in effects, try Bas Relief in conjunction with one or more other filters.

1, 2 Start with a blank file at least as large as the image that you want to treat (this one is 1500 pixels square), and fill it with 50% gray. Go to **Filter > Pixelate > Color Halftone** and increase the default pixel radius to around 50. Hit OK.

3 Select the Bas Relief filter with high Detail (12) and medium–low Smoothness (4). This time, set the direction to Bottom Right. Hit OK. Save this document as a Photoshop (.psd) file, preferably in grayscale mode, and use it in conjunction with Displace, Glass, or, as here, the Texturizer filter.

4, 5 Go to **Filter > Texture > Texturizer**, and click on the arrow next to the Texture menu to reveal the Load Texture command. This will bring up windows by which you can navigate to load the texture that you just created and saved.

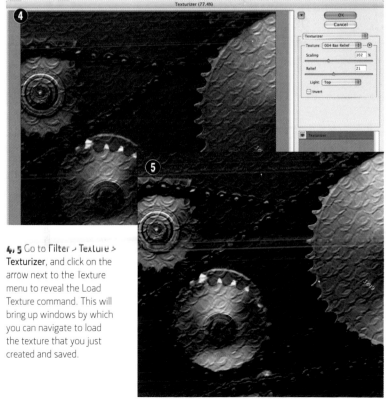

Chalk & Charcoal

This filter applies two sets of directional strokes over a mid-gray background. The charcoal lines—the foreground color—run diagonally from top left to bottom right, and the chalk lines—the background color—run along the opposite axis. The coarse chalk strokes replace the existing highlights and midtones in the image, while the shadows get a charcoal treatment. To get closer to the real thing, try a little handwork after the event with the Smudge tool.

How it works

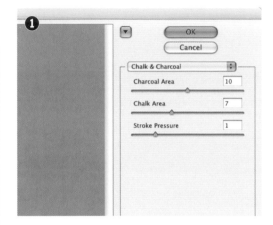

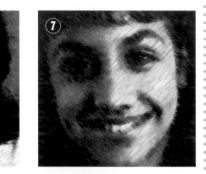

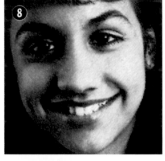

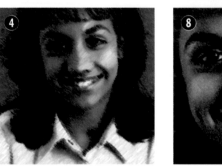

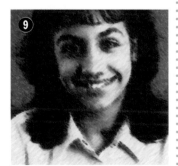

1, 2 The panel's three sliders control the ratio of charcoal to chalk and the strength of application. At these moderate settings, the Chalk & Charcoal filter offers a halfway convincing effect.

3 Maximize both charcoal and chalk (leave stroke pressure at 1) to get a more aggressive overall texture.

4, 5 Try also maximizing charcoal with no value for chalk, then vice-versa.

6 Increase the Stroke Pressure and equalize the Chalk Area and Charcoal Area values for a more "sketchy" result.

7, 8 Although you can alter stroke pressure, the basic pixel size of the "brushes" can't be changed. The source image used in these examples is around 450 pixels wide, but reverting to its original size of around 1500 pixels wide and applying the filter produces quite a different result. Compare the closeup of small (7) and large (8) images.

9 As with the Bas Relief filter, changing the color palette will give different effects. Make sure, however, that your "chalk" is always lighter than your "charcoal," or the effect won't quite be what you expected.

This technique simulates the effect of drawing with a broad-tip marker pen.

1, 2 Duplicate the existing image layer (Ctrl/Cmd+J). Select all, and hit Ctrl/Cmd+T to enter Free Transform mode. Hold down Shift, then click and drag the bottom-right handle toward the top left of the window until the dragged image is about a third of its original size. Release the selection and hit OK to confirm. Leave the selection active.

5, 6 Change the filtered layer's blending mode to Overlay, keeping the opacity at 100%.

3 Open the Chalk & Charcoal filter and apply it at low values: Charcoal Area 4, Chalk Area 4, and Stroke Pressure 2.

4 Hit Ctrl/Cmd+I once more and drag the selection back to its original size, while holding down Shift. Let go when it's in the right place, hit OK, and deselect.

133

7, 8 More variations are available by changing the blending mode again—these are changed to Vivid Light and Luminosity respectively.

Charcoal

The Charcoal filter looks for the principal image edges and applies a thinner or thicker charcoal stroke depending on your settings. The stroke lacks the granularity of the charcoal element of the preceding filter, Chalk & Charcoal. The background color represents the paper in this filter, with diagonal foreground charcoal strokes sketched over the top.

How it works

1 At settings of Charcoal Thickness 6, Detail 3, and Light/Dark Balance 50 the result is a bit too heavy on the charcoal.

2 For a more delicate result, reduce the Charcoal Thickness to minimum, set Detail to 4, and Light/Dark Balance to 80.

3 Try the color change maneuver. Here, a dark blue foreground sets the stroke color while the cream background setting provides the solid "paper."

Using the Charcoal filter

This filter works well with defined edges, but needs to be moderated after the first application.

1, 2 Duplicate the layer (Ctrl/Cmd+J) and run the Charcoal filter using Charcoal Thickness 6, Detail 2, and Light/Dark Balance 70.

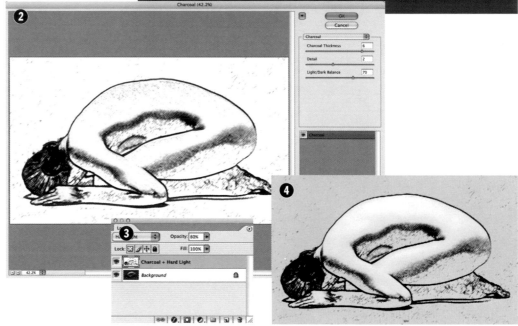

3, 4, 5 Change the layer's blending mode to Luminosity and reduce its opacity to 80%. Another approach is to duplicate the layer and change its blending mode to the little-used Dissolve, to imitate stray fragments of (pink) charcoal.

134

Graphic Pen

This rather harsh treatment, like Chrome, needs softening after application. The necessarily high-contrast effect demands a strongly structured subject. Interesting results can be obtained by changing the default black and white palette to a less severe combination—try a mid-brown foreground on a light-brown background.

How it works

1, 2 Juggle the two sliders for a balanced effect—there's generally only a narrow band of settings that will work successfully.

3 Here the color palette has been reset to dark and light blue, and the stroke direction changed to horizontal.

Using the Graphic Pen filter

The stark effect of Graphic Pen is best kept under control by confining it to individual channels and subsequently altering blending modes.

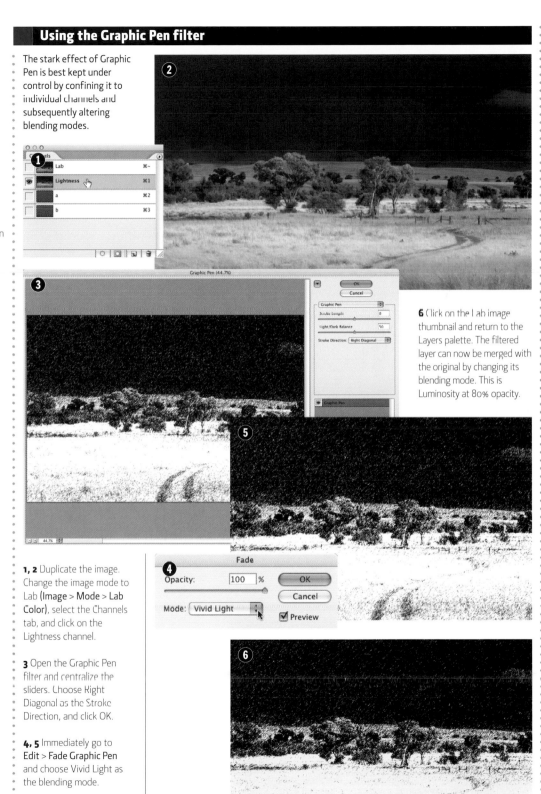

6 Click on the Lab image thumbnail and return to the Layers palette. The filtered layer can now be merged with the original by changing its blending mode. This is Luminosity at 80% opacity.

1, 2 Duplicate the image. Change the image mode to Lab (**Image > Mode > Lab Color**), select the Channels tab, and click on the Lightness channel.

3 Open the Graphic Pen filter and centralize the sliders. Choose Right Diagonal as the Stroke Direction, and click OK.

4, 5 Immediately go to **Edit > Fade Graphic Pen** and choose Vivid Light as the blending mode.

You see the effects of the Chrome filter in a lot of Photoshop work these days. It differs from the familiar hubcap illusion in that the reflections are generated by and within the filtered image itself, rather than from the outside world. The effect is often too powerful and erratic to be used undiluted, and we'll examine some strategies to calm it down. The Photoshop manual recommends immediate adjustment with the Levels command, though this is not in itself a sufficient remedy. Unlike most of the filters in the Sketch suite, changes in the color palette have no effect.

How it works

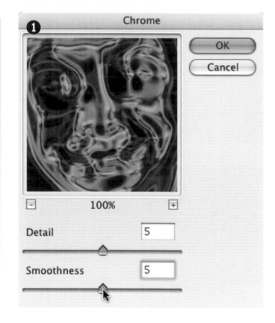

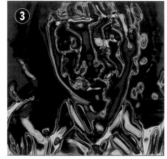

1, 2 The two sliders control detail and smoothness. Even at medium settings the image is effectively destroyed. It's also clear that the Preview provided doesn't resemble the finished effect.

3 Even with both sliders at zero there's little remaining of the original structure.

Using the Chrome filter

This technique involves a progressive application of the Chrome filter in order to reduce the number of reflection points.

1, 2 Duplicate the original layer and Shift+click to select the background, with the Magic Wand tool set to a medium tolerance.

3, 4 When you have completely selected the background, invert the selection (Ctrl/Cmd+Shift+I) to select the head. Click on the mask icon at the foot of the Layers palette to add a layer mask. The mask thumbnail will appear alongside the image thumbnail, surrounded by a rectangle to indicate that it is active. The mask doesn't need any more work, so click on the image thumbnail to make it active instead.

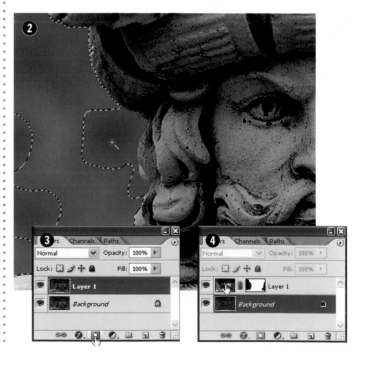

136

5 Select the Lasso tool and give it a large feather radius. As a guide, this image is 2000 pixels wide and the selected lasso feather radius is 40 pixels. Start selecting small areas of the head. The easiest method is to hold down the Alt/Option key and click from point to point rather than drawing freehand. In any case, great precision is not required; the background is protected by the mask and any over- or underlap is easily fixed as the work progresses.

6 Apply the Chrome filter to the selected area with minimum Detail and maximum Smoothness. Deselect and capture another section.

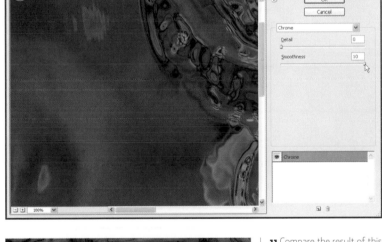

7, 8 Continue in this way, selecting progressively smaller sections and filtering (just hit Ctrl/Cmd+F), until the head is complete. Use a smaller Lasso radius for the more detailed sections.

9, 10 Finally, go to **Image** > **Adjustments** > **Levels** and move the Input sliders toward the center to create a more stark effect. You can also use the Lighten tool to relieve dark areas if necessary.

11 Compare the result of this ten-step process with that achieved with one overall application of the filter.

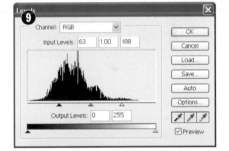

137

Halftone Pattern

Halftone Pattern arrived in the Sketch suite in ancient Photoshop history. Rather than attempt to reproduce true halftone screening in the way that the Color Halftone filter does (see page 104), this filter overlays a pattern on the image and alters its colors to reflect the current foreground and background. The Pattern Type settings are interesting, with Circle giving a not-quite-what-you-expected concentric effect, and Line replicating an interleaved TV screen. The Dot and Line settings are more useful for introducing a mechanical atmosphere. Change the background color in the palette to a pastel shade to simulate a colored paper ground.

How it works

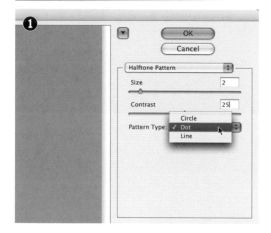

1,2 With a small original like this one, you need to choose a small size. The same applies if you choose the Circle or Line options.

3, 4 Raise the Contrast to maximum for the typical hard halftone effect, and increase Size for something more radical.

5 Alter the color palette for a little sub-Warholia.

6 You may only need the Circle pattern twice in a lifetime, but it's comforting to know it's there.

7 The Line pattern is more useful, especially in conjunction with other techniques (see the following example).

8, 9 If you choose a plain 50% gray as your target, you can produce useful screen and dot rulings for use on other images. Here the dot pattern has been enlarged so that the dots merge into a checkerboard pattern. The second example has the line pattern at maximum contrast.

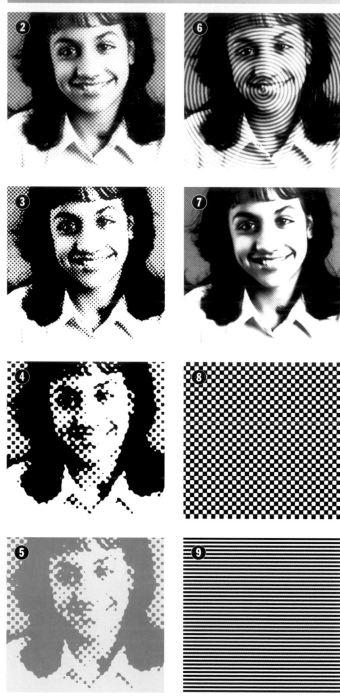

138

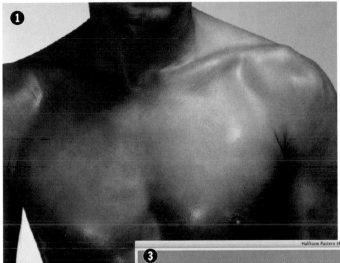

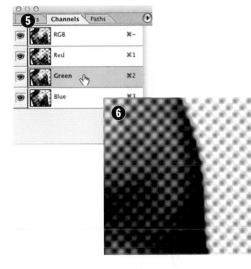

5, 6, 7 Repeat the process on the Green and Blue channels. Click on the Green channel to activate it, but also click to see the eyeball next to the RGB icon. Zoom in close on the image. Hold

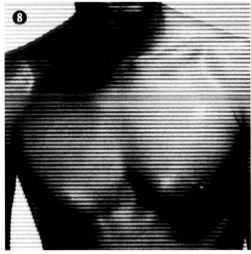

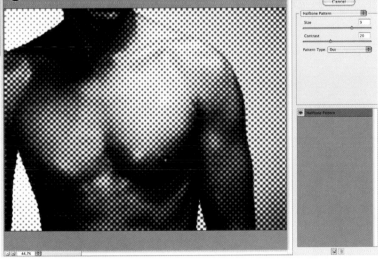

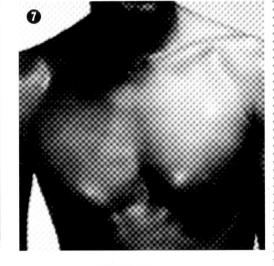

Sitting too close to the TV screen is bad for your eyes, as every young child has been told. Fortunately, we can harmlessly replicate the effect of millions of red, blue and green glowing phosphor dots using the Halftone Pattern filter. Do not adjust your set.

1,2 Ensure your image is in RGB mode and go to the Channels palette. Click on the Red channel.

3, 4 Open the Halftone filter. Select Size 9, Contrast 20, and choose Dot as the pattern type. The idea is to get a slightly soft, round-edged shape by juggling the sliders. Hit OK.

down the Ctrl/Cmd key and use the arrow keys to nudge the Green channel slightly downward and, by the same amount, to the left. Do the same for the Blue channel, but downward and to the right. The final task is to trim away the few pixels at the edges of the image.

8 Here we're using the same filtration but with Line as the pattern, nudging each of the channels a little, then treating them with a small amount of **Filter > Distort > Ocean Ripple** (see page 71).

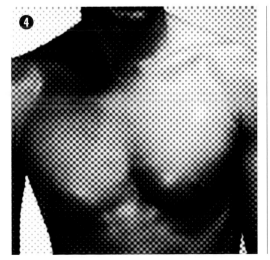

139

Note Paper

The Note Paper filter combines the functions of the Emboss filter from the Stylize suite and Grain from the Texture suite, and gives a striking result, though perhaps one of restricted usefulness. Note Paper's intended illusion is that of a paper layer with holes that coincide with dark image areas, revealing a second layer below. Increase the Image Balance slider to cut away more of the top layer.

How it works

1 Move all three sliders to zero, then drag the Image Balance slider to pick up a selection of the dark component of the image. These areas will eventually appear transparent.

2 Gradually increase the Relief value to produce a shadow edge.

3 Finally, increase the Grain slider to introduce some texture into the image.

Using the Note Paper filter

Try finely adjusting the Image Balance control to take advantage of Note Paper's stratifying properties.

1, 2 Duplicate the image three or four times and open the Note Paper filter for use on the top layer. Move the Image Balance control so that you see only a small part of the image.

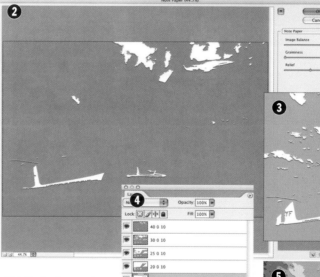

3 Hide the top layer and move to the next layer down. Run the filter as before, but reduce the Image Balance value, thus revealing more of the image.

4 Continue down through the layers, or until you have all image and no background.

5 Change all the layers' blending modes to Linear Burn at 50% opacity—don't alter the base layer. This example is five layers deep.

6 To re-establish some color, go to **Image > Adjustments > Hue/Saturation** and choose Colorize. Adjust Hue separately for each layer.

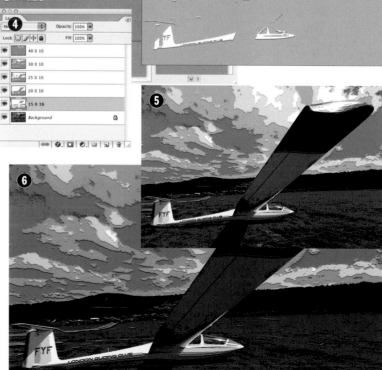

140

Photocopy

Years before the Photocopy filter was designed, photocopiers gave off poisonous fumes and made the lights go dim, but the resulting damp sheet of paper, though only a rough approximation of the original, was a marvel—and well worth simulating in Photoshop. Modern photocopiers are much more accurate than this filter would suggest. However, if you disregard its original purpose, this filter makes an excellent starting point for impromptu poster effects.

How it works

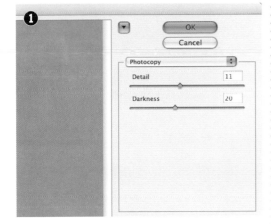

1,2 At an arbitrary first setting, it's so real you can almost smell the ammonia. This effect could come in handy for replicating a gritty, punk-rock fanzine look.

Using the Photocopy filter

At the highest settings, Photocopy can produce some useful high-contrast effects for combination with the source image.

1,2 Duplicate the background layer, then open the Photocopy filter and apply it at maximum intensity.

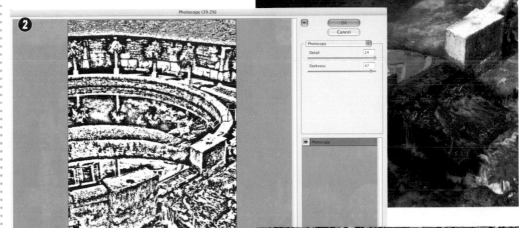

3, 4 The result is not very useful on its own, but can be blended—here with Linear Burn—with the source image to produce a colored wood-block effect.

Plaster

A mix between the Note Paper and Bas Relief filters, Plaster attempts a molded transformation and artfully adds light and shadow reminiscent of the Emboss filter. The Image Balance slider controls how much of the image is raised from the base.

How it works

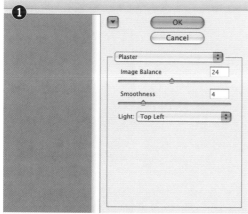

1, 2 With the default color palette in use, the lighter areas of the image are raised against a black ground.

3 Increasing the Smoothness value renders the image even more enigmatic.

4 Try varying both foreground and background colors for a softer result.

Using the Plaster filter

Try this not-quite-cameo technique on family portraits. Full periwig and frogging are not obligatory.

1, 2, 3 Duplicate the image twice. Click on the foreground color in the palette to choose a new light brown color. Click OK. Working on the top layer, use the Magic Wand to select the background, then invert the selection (Ctrl/Cmd+Shift+I).

4 Run the Plaster filter, and manipulate the sliders to get the clearest rendering of the subject's features.

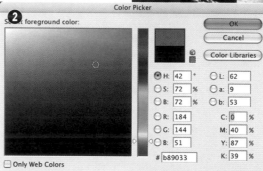

5 With the selection still active, hide the top layer and work on the next layer. Choose a different, related color in the Picker as a new foreground color. Run the Plaster filter again, but reduce the Image Balance value. Hit Backspace to delete the background from both layers, then deselect.

6, 7 Move up to work on the top layer. Set its blending mode to Linear Burn and click on the Layer Styles icon at the foot of the palette. When the dialog box opens, choose Bevel and Emboss, change Structure to Inner Bevel and Smooth, and experiment with the position of the Shading light by clicking

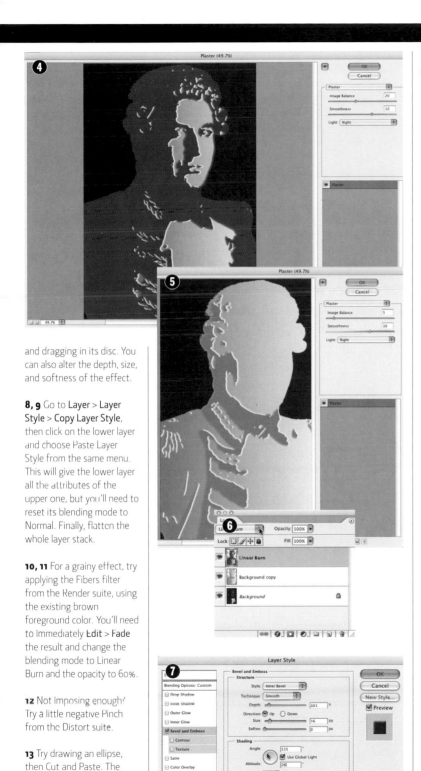

and dragging in its disc. You can also alter the depth, size, and softness of the effect.

8, 9 Go to **Layer > Layer Style > Copy Layer Style**, then click on the lower layer and choose **Paste Layer Style** from the same menu. This will give the lower layer all the attributes of the upper one, but you'll need to reset its blending mode to Normal. Finally, flatten the whole layer stack.

10, 11 For a grainy effect, try applying the Fibers filter from the Render suite, using the existing brown foreground color. You'll need to immediately **Edit > Fade** the result and change the blending mode to Linear Burn and the opacity to 60%.

12 Not imposing enough? Try a little negative Pinch from the Distort suite.

13 Try drawing an ellipse, then Cut and Paste. The selection will make a new layer. Hide the background layer and go once again to the Layer Styles dialog. You can start with the settings

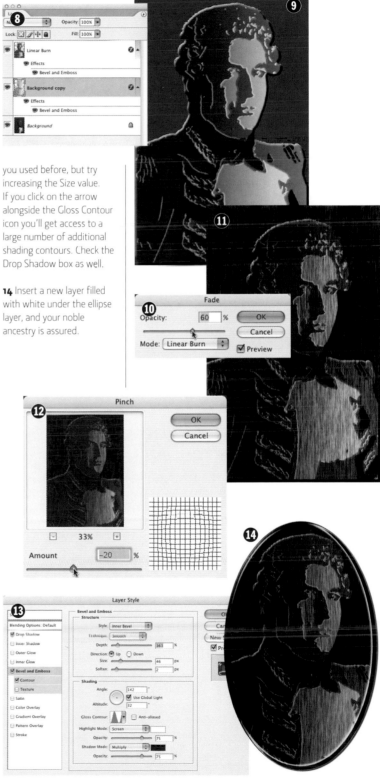

you used before, but try increasing the Size value. If you click on the arrow alongside the Gloss Contour icon you'll get access to a large number of additional shading contours. Check the Drop Shadow box as well.

14 Insert a new layer filled with white under the ellipse layer, and your noble ancestry is assured.

Reticulation

The characteristic "crazed" pattern of film reticulation was a daily hazard in developing silver-based film in the early years of photography. During processing, the thin layer of emulsion would stretch or shrink at a different rate than the glass or cellulose-based support. It ceased to be an issue with plastic-based film supports, but lives on in photographic legend. The Photoshop filter faithfully reproduces the termite-like trails of severe reticulation.

How it works

1 The filter has a preset pattern of "termite trails," seen here at 200% enlargement.

2 Try moderate settings at first—it's difficult to find a setting for portrait use that looks healthy.

3 Ironically, one of the most satisfactory settings seems to be one with all of the sliders set to zero.

Using the Reticulation filter

Reticulation is typical of the filters containing preset patterns that can be usefully combined with others. In this example, Plastic Wrap is the companion.

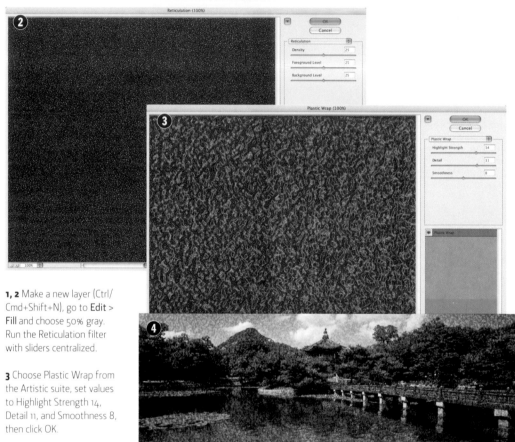

1, 2 Make a new layer (Ctrl/Cmd+Shift+N), go to **Edit > Fill** and choose 50% gray. Run the Reticulation filter with sliders centralized.

3 Choose Plastic Wrap from the Artistic suite, set values to Highlight Strength 14, Detail 11, and Smoothness 8, then click OK.

4,5 Change the blending mode of the upper layer to Overlay and reduce its opacity to 80%. The close-up clearly shows a soap-bubble pattern.

6 You can use this combination pattern as an alpha channel texture map in Lighting Effects as well (see page 118).

Stamp

The Stamp filter produces extreme contrast and allows for control of edge simplification. The Stamp engine forms the basis for the Note Paper and Plaster effects, but it is perhaps a little too stark when left on its own. Its supposed affinity with wood or rubber stamps is not apparent in one-shot use. If you're looking for the characteristic strike of wooden type, for example, try a grayscale scan of some real timber and blend it with your original. For a rubber-stamp squash, duplicate your picture, nudge both copies around slightly with the Smudge tool and combine them using the Overlay blending mode.

How it works

1 The Light/Dark balance slider runs from solid white to solid black. Smoothness has to be kept at a low value to avoid the total destruction of the image.

2, 3 With the Smoothness slider increased to 8, the image is on its way to obscurity, which it finally reaches with a setting of 14.

Using the Stamp filter

To increase the possibilities of the one-dimensional Stamp filter, some intervention is necessary.

1, 2 For a three-color result, duplicate the image twice. Insert a blank layer filled with white at the bottom of the layer stack. Run the filter on the top layer with low Smoothness, retaining as much detail as possible.

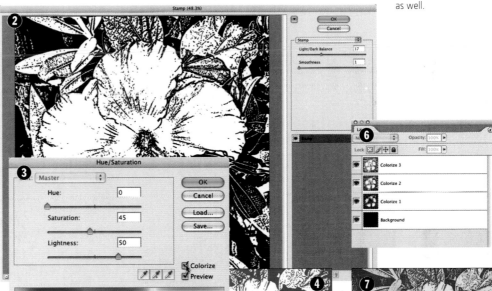

3 Colorize the layer using Image > Adjustments > Hue/Saturation (check the Colorize box). This setting results in a red-brown. Hit OK, hide this layer, and activate the next one down.

4 Increasing the Light/Dark Balance value gathers up more of the image; increasing Smoothness simplifies the shapes. When you're done, hit OK and colorize this layer to a different shade.

5 Turn to the last layer and apply Stamp with raised values for both Light/Dark Balance and Smoothness.

Almost all detail will be lost except for strong highlights. Colorize this layer as well.

6, 7, 8 Fill the white layer with a dark color—here it's a dark purple. Change the opacity of all three image layers to 60%. For an alternative, try changing all of the layer blending modes to Color Burn— you'll need to lighten and re-colorize the base layer as well.

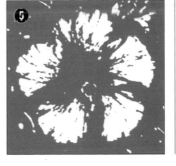

145

Torn Edges

The Torn Edges filter is very similar to the Stamp filter, but with rough edges as opposed to Stamp's stark, clean lines. There is also an additional Contrast control that modifies the graininess and the contrast of the image.

How it works

1, 2 With the Smoothness slider at medium, there is some softening of the high-contrast edges, but no sign of tearing. Increasing Smoothness and Contrast in tandem leads to destruction of the image detail.

3 You can also try changing the foreground and background colors. It's an interesting effect, but the edges still just look fuzzy rather that torn.

A better way to create torn edges

If you do need to simulate torn edges, here's a workaround that avoids using the Torn Edges filter.

1, 2 Insert a new light gray layer under your image. Use the Lasso tool, set to a 1-pixel feather, to draw around the area to be cut away, then hit Ctrl/Cmd+X to cut it.

3 Work along the resulting edge with the Smudge tool set to maximum hardness.

4, 5, 6 Select the background area with the Magic Wand tool. With this selection active, go to the Paths palette, click on the fly-out button, and choose Make Work Path. When the dialog appears, just hit OK.

7 Select the Eraser tool and go to the Brush Presets tab—normally docked in the palette well in the Tool Options bar. Choose Rough Round Bristle—third from last in the default brush collection, and drag the slider to reduce its diameter.

8, 9, 10 Return to the Paths palette fly-out button and go to Stroke Path. Choose Eraser in the subsequent dialog box and hit OK. You may need to stroke the path more than once to clean the edge. Add a drop shadow to make the edge more emphatic using the Layer Styles dialog—click on the F symbol at the foot of the Layers palette and experiment with the settings in the resulting dialog until you're happy with the result.

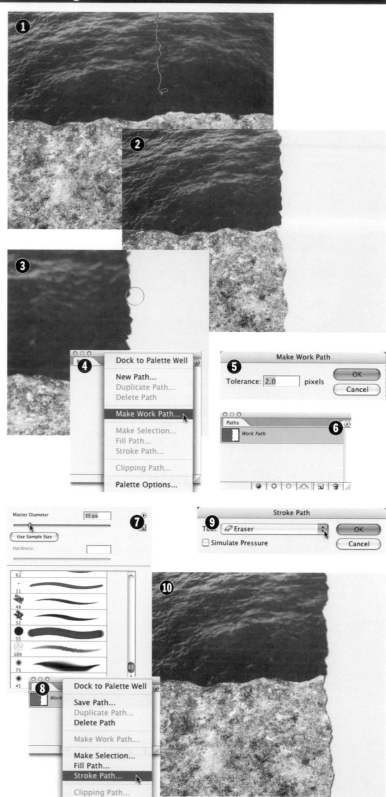

Water Paper

An alternative approach to Watercolor (in the Artistic suite), Water Paper contains a rectilinear fiber pattern. Real watercolor pigment tends to pool in the tiny gaps between the paper fibers, leaving lighter areas atop the fibers themselves. This filter attempts to approximate this effect by bleeding image colors along the fiber axes. The foreground and background colors have no effect on this filter.

How it works

1 The filter is equipped with preset paper fibers, seen here at 200% enlargement.

2 At minimum Fiber Length, an interesting pattern develops, shown here at 200% enlargement.

3 Increasing fiber length to 10 brings in a strong network of black crosshatching. At length 20 the image is in trouble, and no amount of manipulation of brightness or contrast can rescue it.

An alternative to the Water Paper filter

One method of simulating water(color) paper involves the Texturizer filter in the Texture suite (see page 168). Alternatively, to simulate watercolor painting you can use the Watercolor filter (page 37). Here, though, we'll experiment with the little-used Art History brush.

1, 2, 3 Select the Art History brush from the Toolbar. Settings for the Art History brush are made in the Tool Options bar. The most useful brush styles are the three Tight options—the others, except for the nervous Dab, are only good for very late Van Gogh.

4, 5 If you haven't used the Art History brush before, open the document you're going to work on and then open the History palette. Click on the small black arrow at the top right of the palette and select New Snapshot. Hit OK in the resulting window. Next, duplicate the image so you have an untreated version as a reference point. From this point on, you will need a strong sense of commitment to your task, because if you decide to save and close the document, the relevant history state will be lost and you'll have to start over from the beginning. Now fill the duplicate image with any solid color by selecting **Edit > Fill**. The source state for the brush will, by default, be the image's state when first opened. Take up the brush—it's set to 20-pixels diameter

and 0% hardness by default—and begin scribbling in the void. This is a good opportunity to make a long phone call as there's no particular technique involved; the "art" image will gradually appear as you work.

6 The image will change with each pass of the brush. This was the result of 20 minutes spent scribbling roughly over the image, then changing to the slightly more intricate Tight Short brush for the details.

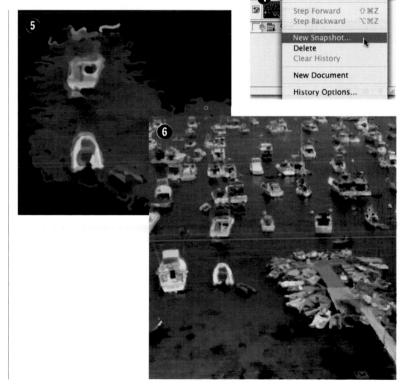

The Stylize filters

Like their immediate predecessors in the Sketch suite, the nine filters in the Stylize suite are often used more for effect than enhancement, but they can be of use to the photographer. The Stylize filters tend to work on high-contrast boundaries and edges in an image, rather than plain expanses of color. Diffuse breaks up and softens edges; Emboss, as its name suggests, makes your images look like they've been stamped in metal; and Extrude makes your images explode in a mass of pyramids or cuboids. Find Edges (which should perhaps more properly be called Emphasize Edges) and Glowing Edges offer strongly surreal effects that usually need to be moderated, but can work very well with other filters. Their neighbors are a motley crew: Solarize has its history in trickery with reversal color transparency film; Tiles is (or are) apparently misplaced, with its true home alongside Mosaic Tiles and Craquelure in the Texture suite; Trace Contour produces multicolored lines along image edges; and finally, Wind brings up the rear, pining for its true companions, Wave and Motion Blur.

The Stylize filters

page 149—Diffuse

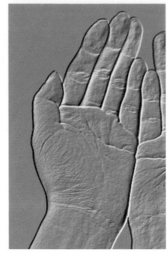

page 150—Emboss

page 151—Glowing Edges

page 152—Extrude

page 153—Find Edges

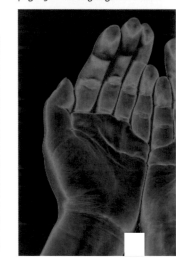

page 154—Solarize

page 155—Tiles

page 156—Trace Contour

page 158—Wind

Diffuse

The four modes of the Diffuse filter shift pixels at strong edges in the image. The first three leave distinct pixelation traces along the boundaries, with Normal shuffling all pixels, Darken Only replacing light pixels with dark pixels, and Lighten Only doing exactly the opposite. The last option, Anisotropic, moves the pixels according to the smallest change in color, and gives a smooth effect, quite different than the results of the first three options. All four would be more useful with a variable intensity control, but as they are, they serve to break up image edges ready for subsequent alteration.

How it works

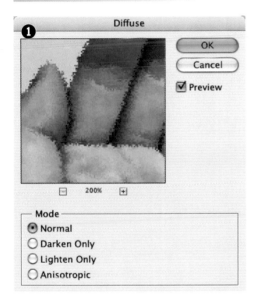

1 The panel offers four types of shifting based on a search for contrasting edges within the image.

2 Normal moves pixels around randomly at the discovered edges (here enlarged to 200%).

3, 4 Darken Edges adds only darker pixels, while Lighten does the opposite.

5 Anisotropic mode shuffles pixels toward the areas of least color change.

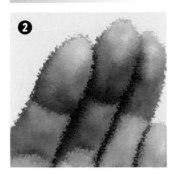

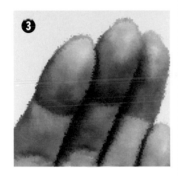

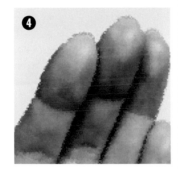

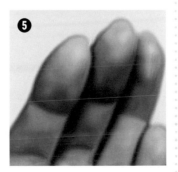

Using the Diffuse filter

While one application of the Diffuse filter on a large image may not have a significant effect, ten or more may do the trick.

1, 2, 3 The source image is around 2400 pixels wide. With just one application of Diffuse in Normal mode, there is not a great deal of change. The only real noticeable difference is in the areas with distinct edges, such as the tree line against the sky.

4 Hover over the Ctrl/Cmd and F keys and hit them 10 times to repeat the filtration—or 20, if you're feeling really adventurous.

149

Emboss

Very similar in effect to Bas Relief in the Sketch suite, Emboss offers superior 360° control of lighting direction, but dispenses with the texture function. Its severe effect can be useful, although it's best at low settings with subsequent fading. Larger Height values reveal the mechanics behind the filter—light and dark versions of the image are created and simply overlaid to create the 3D effect.

How it works

1 The panel offers Angle, Height, and Amount controls. Except on very large images, the pixel heights offered are wildly destructive. At 1 pixel Height and 15% Amount, the image is just becoming visible. With a little more treatment, this could simulate a watermark.

2 Increasing the Amount setting to 100% gives a more distinct outline, but the image is still securely anchored in fog.

3 At the maximum 500% Amount setting, the characteristic spectral edges are very clear.

Using the Emboss filter

Try this for a simple two-and-a-half dimensional effect that sidesteps the complications of the Lighting Effects filter.

1, 2 Open the Emboss filter and choose a small Height value, and medium Amount.

3, 4 Immediately go to **Edit > Fade Emboss** and choose Overlay as the blending mode, but leave opacity at 100%. The resulting effect is just plausible as a shot made in the camera.

5 For a more surreal effect, go back to the original and apply the Emboss filter exactly as before, but this time choose Difference as the blending mode.

6, 7 To restore the raised rather than incised appearance, return to the original image, invert the color values (Ctrl/Cmd+I), and then run the Emboss filter and fade with Difference as before.

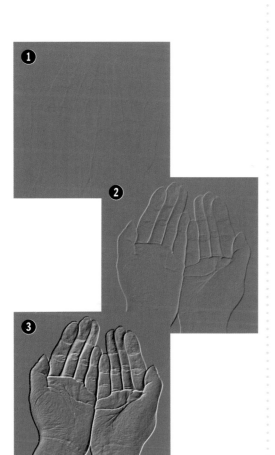

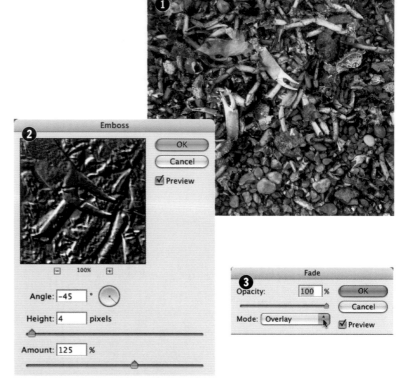

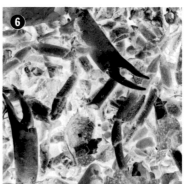

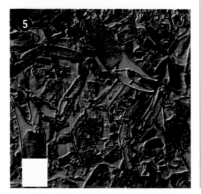

Glowing Edges

The effect of Glowing Edges is very similar to Find Edges (see page 153) in reverse. Try both on the same subject, and invert one. The images will be almost identical. The difference is that Glowing Edges offers three different controls for varying the effect, whereas Find Edges is a one-shot job. Another difference is that Glowing Edges is the only filter in the Stylize group that can be used with the Filter Gallery, allowing quick combinations with various other filter effects.

How it works

1, 2 Glowing Edges inverts the image's tonal values before applying the same treatment as Find Edges.

3 Still at Edge Width 2, pushing the other two sliders to maximum gives a bizarre musculoskeletal effect that wouldn't look out of place in the movie *Tron*.

Using the Glowing Edges filter

Although Glowing Edges is usually used for its dramatic treatment of colored lines against a black ground, it can also produce an interesting, soft, "painted" effect.

1, 2, 3 One direct application of the filter set at Edge Width 3, Edge Brightness 12, and Smoothness 15 gives the expected network of lines.

4, 5, 6 Step back to the original and give it a small amount of Gaussian Blur at 10 pixels Radius, then re-run the Glowing Edges filter at the original settings. Immediately fade the result using Screen blending mode.

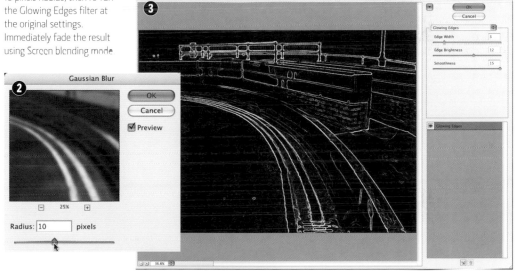

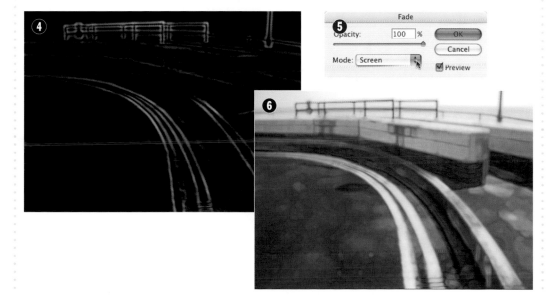

151

Extrude

The Extrude filter divides an image into squares and then extrudes (pulls out) these squares to form 3D columns. The columns can either be capped with the original image, or a solid color based on the average color of the pixels of that square. The sides of the columns are always made up of solid color. The columns extend out as if from a sphere, so the central columns point almost directly toward the viewer, while the more peripheral columns are at more of an angle. The Pyramid option creates pyramids rather than square columns, with the four sides filled with solid color. The Mask Incomplete Blocks option removes columns at the image edges that would normally extend outside the image area.

How it works

1 The controls are basic and lack a preview window. Solid Front Face averages the color in, for example, a 30-pixel-square area and plants the result on top of the block. Mask Incomplete Blocks will suppress any blocks that might break the edge of a selected area. The Random setting produces blocks of arbitrary height.

2 With Solid Front Faces unchecked, the image arrives unaltered on top of the blocks.

3 With Solid Front Faces checked, but with Level-based selected instead of Random, the blocks are highest where the source image is lightest.

4 Pyramids repeats the exercise, though Solid Front Faces is inevitably the only image option available.

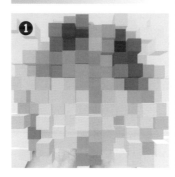

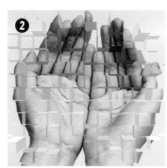

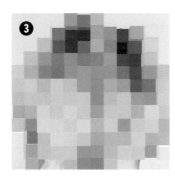

Using the Extrude filter

The Pyramid function of this filter can be exploited to make patterns. They can be used directly as patterns, as texture maps, or as backgrounds for existing images.

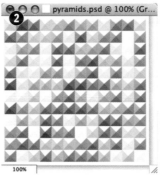

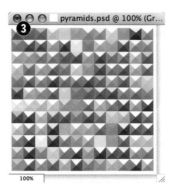

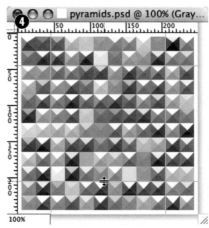

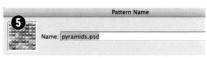

1 Make a new grayscale document 250 pixels square (use the same resolution you use for your normal images), and make sure Background is set to White or Background Color. Name it Pyramids. Open the Extrude filter and choose Pyramids. Set the filter as here and hit OK.

2, 3 The result may look a little pale, so hit Ctrl/Cmd-F to repeat the filter.

4 Since the pixel height setting was very low, there is little perspective distortion in this "overhead" view, though if you look in the corners and along the edges you'll see a slight bowing outwards. Make Rulers visible (in the View menu) and drag out some guides to aid in cropping off the edges of the image. Set **Snap To > Guides**, also in the View menu, and use the Crop tool to trim the image. Go to **View > Clear Guides**.

5 Go to the Edit menu and choose Define Pattern. The dialog box opens with the name of the file already in place. Hit OK.

6, 7 Open the image you want to treat with the pyramid pattern. Go to **Edit > Fill** and choose Pattern. Click on the blue area to the side of the Custom pattern window, and then on the newly created pattern. Hit OK.

8, 9 Immediately go to **Edit > Fade** and choose Overlay as the blend. Here, the filter's opacity has also been changed to 80%.

152

Find Edges

True to its name, Find Edges finds edges. Having done so, it calculates the adjacent colors and draws a line. The color of the line is dependent on the relative brightness of the adjacent colors. Experiment with different blending modes and opacities using the Edit > Fade Find Edges command immediately after application.

How it works

Find Edges offers interesting possibilities for multiple overlays.

1, 2 Duplicate the image twice, to make three identical layers. Run the filter on the top layer.

3, 4, 5 Leave the top layer visible, and change its blending mode to Soft Light. Make the middle layer active, and run the Find Edges filter. Change this layer's blending mode to Hue. The closeup shows a combination of outline and spectral effects.

6 For a lighter, more painterly appearance, invert the middle layer and change its blending mode to Screen.

7 For more intense color and heavy white outlines, invert the top layer as well.

Using the Find Edges filter

Solarize

Solarize attempts to mimic a rather complex photographic maneuver. Real solarization of photographic emulsion (in prints, negatives, and transparencies) is achieved by exposing and partially developing the image, then subjecting it to a second, all-over, fogging exposure. Development is then resumed, giving the characteristic tone reversal in some, but not all, areas of the image. The filter has no settings—try using Hue/Saturation afterwards to get a greater variety of color combinations.

How it works

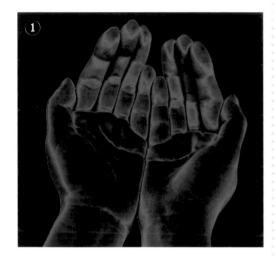

There's only one flavor of Solarize.

1 This is it. For more variety, use the Curves function— see the following example.

Using Curves to achieve a solarization effect

To get close to a simulation of real reversal film solarization, we need to look further afield than the Solarize filter.

1, 2, 3 Open Image > Adjustments > Curves and modify the existing straight graph line by clicking on its length to add more anchor points. Drag the points, switchback-style, up and down while watching the effect on the source image.

4 If your image ends up like this, you've probably overdone the switchbacking.

5, 6 A monochromatic image can also be manipulated in this fashion.

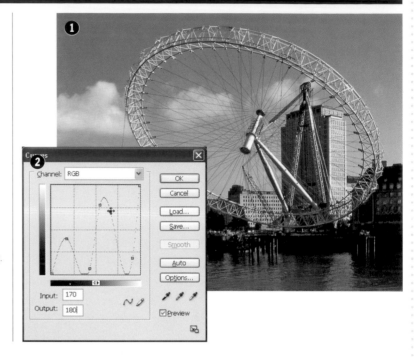

Tiles

Laying mosaic tiles neatly is not very difficult—and even less so if you're using Photoshop. The Number of Tiles box allows you to define the number of tiles that appear vertically in the image. The tiles are always square, so Photoshop will calculate the size of the tiles according to the number that you specify, and repeat them across the entire image or selection area. The Maximum Offset function allows you to control the amount of movement of each tile, with a range from "very precise" to "Romans in a big hurry!" Unfortunately, the function can only displace the tiles vertically and horizontally—you can't add rotation.

How it works

1 You can vary the Number of Tiles and their degree of Offset in any amount between 1 and 99.

2 Choose your grout color (Fill Empty Areas) carefully.

Sometimes colored grout will work better than black or white.

3 Choose Invert Image or Unaltered Image to repeat the image in the background.

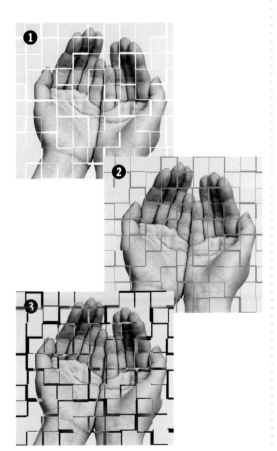

Using the Tiles filter

Give the Tiles filter a boost with Layer Styles.

1, 2 Set the color palette to default (Key D) and open the Tiles filter. Set the requested numbers and Foreground Color to fill the gaps between the tiles.

3 Choose the Magic Wand with Contiguous unchecked, and click in a black area. With the selection active, invert it (Ctrl/Cmd+Shift+I), then Cut and Paste. A new layer will appear, with the tile image only. Deselect and return to the base layer, and fill it with black.

4, 5 Return to the tiled layer and call up Layer Styles (Layer > Layer Style > Bevel & Emboss or click on the symbol at the foot of the Layers palette). There are many options—and if you click on Contour in the left-hand column, there are even more. The most critical controls are the Angle disc—click and drag on it to change the lighting direction and altitude—and the Size slider, where less is generally better than more.

6, 7 You can use the Eraser, set to a small hard tip, to introduce cracks and detailing in the tiles, as well as to separate tiles the filter has left joined together, or else use the Marquee tool to select and delete entire tiles. All of these deletions will automatically acquire a beveled edge, courtesy of the Layer Style.

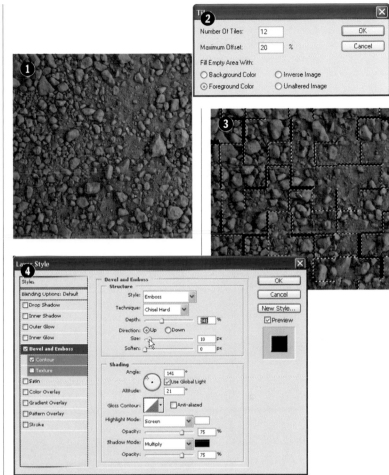

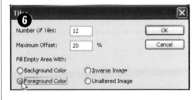

155

Trace Contour

Trace Contour looks at relative brightness levels rather than the usual contrast edges, and surrounds similar areas with a one-pixel-wide line. For a good example of the filter in action, try running it on a simple black-to-white gradient. When you move the Threshold slider, you can clearly see the difference it makes, moving from the dark areas at a low Threshold value to light areas at higher Threshold values. As with Find Edges and Glowing Edges, it's best to immediately follow this filter by modifying the blending mode and opacity.

How it works

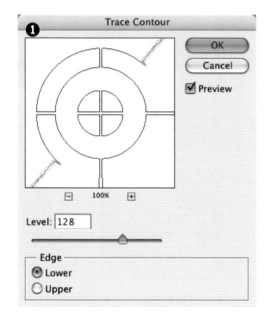

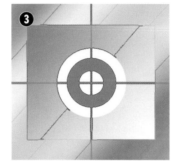

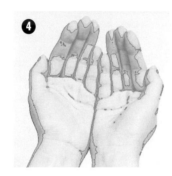

1, 2, 3 The gray gradation on the target image runs from absolute black (0 in brightness terms) to white (255). Running the filter at level 128 (half way) with Lower Edge selected produces a contour halfway across the gradient. The four white quadrants at the target's center are also clearly outlined. Here, the contour lines have been overlaid on a faint version of the target. You can also see contour lines in the color gradients where the brightness level is 128.

4 Selecting Lower Edge shifts the boundary of the detected area to sit within the darker area instead of the lighter. In practical terms, this is of little interest. Colored lines show where contour lines have been created in each of the three color channels (four in CMYK mode). In this composite example in RGB, the cyan lines (on the left side of the left hand) indicate outlines at the 128 level in the Red channel, magenta lines indicate the Green channel, and yellow lines indicate the Blue channel.

This filter often produces a wealth of confusing lines on a white ground when it is used on an RGB image. More interesting results can be found by switching to Lab color mode.

1, 2, 3 Duplicate the background image layer twice (to make three layers in total), then go to **Image > Mode > Lab Color** to change to Lab color mode. Run the Trace Contour filter on the top layer, choosing Lower Edge for a simpler line structure, and a Level value of 200 to outlines the image. Hit OK.

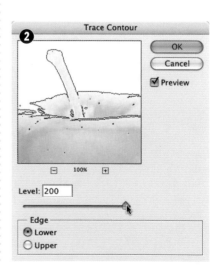

156

4 Hide the top layer, activate the middle layer, and open the Trace Contour filter again. Select a lower Level value—say, 100.

5 Move to the bottom layer and apply a still lower figure—50, in this case.

6, 7 Change the blending mode of the top two layers to Linear Burn.

8 For a final flourish, flatten the image by clicking on the fly-out button at the top right of the Layers palette, and apply the first two filters in the Stylize suite. Use Diffuse with Anisotropic selected to soften the lines a little, followed by Emboss at maximum Height and Amount to produce this effect that's reminiscent of screen printing.

❸

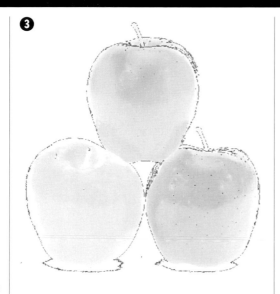

❹

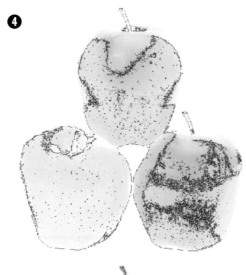

❺

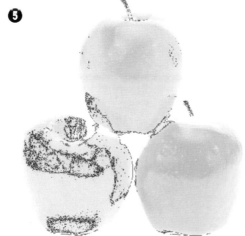

❻

❼

❽

Wind

The Wind filter is more useful for stylization rather than actually reproducing weather effects, hence its inclusion in this filter group. If you are looking for a more realistic alternative, then try Motion Blur (see page 48). Having said that, a light application of this filter faded to a very low opacity can give just a hint of movement to a static image. The Blast and Stagger options are generally not as effective as the Wind option.

How it works

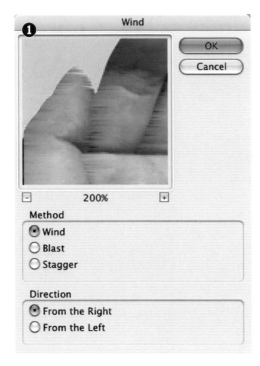

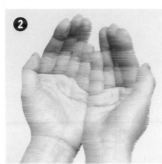

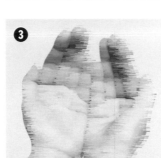

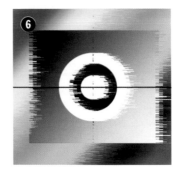

1 The controls for the filter are rudimentary.

2, 3, 4 While Wind and Blast both have reasonably predictable effects, with 1-pixel deep strips being randomly displaced, Stagger attacks the image with considerable force.

5, 6, 7 The target image, with the breeze coming from the left, shows the moderate effect of Wind and Blast, with Stagger displacing pixels and pasting them at the canvas edge.

158

To whip up a halfway realistic blast, you need to assist the limp Wind filter.

1 Outline the top three-quarters of the image with the rectangular marquee, and go to **Select** > **Feather**. This image is 1800 pixels wide, so choose a radius of 200 pixels.

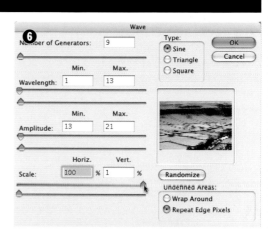

2, 3 Hide the selection (Ctrl/Cmd+H), open the Wind filter, and apply Stagger.

4, 5 Go to **Filter** > **Blur** > **Motion Blur** and apply a small amount of blur at an angle following the axis of the picture.

6, 7, 8, 9 With the selection still active, go to **Filter** > **Distort** > **Wave** and apply very low values. Immediately go to **Edit** > **Fade Wave** and reduce the effect further by changing the blending mode to Linear Burn and reducing the opacity to 30%. Finally, the relics of the Blast filter will need to be cropped away from the left-hand side of the image.

159

The Texture filters

You will find vestiges of ancient arts and artifacts as you enter the Texture suite. For example, craquelure, often seen in antique oil paintings, can be applied to contemporary images to add visual interest. Mosaic and patchwork effects based on age-old traditions can easily be applied. Grainy textures, which digital photographers generally try to eradicate, become a creative tool. You can even create an authentic stained glass effect, although the Stained Glass filter may not be the best way to achieve it (we show you an alternative technique on page 165). And, in addition to the ready-made textures available with the Texturizer filter, you can make your own to create the illusion of a hand-crafted image. The filters in this suite offer plenty of opportunities to explore.

The Texture filters

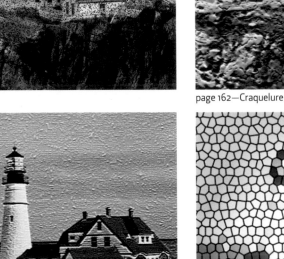

page 161—Grain

page 162—Craquelure

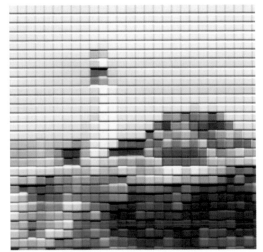

page 164—Mosaic Tiles

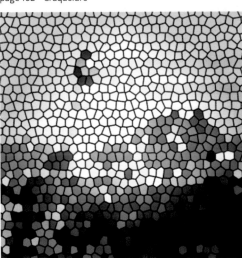

page 165—Stained Glass

page 166—Patchwork

page 168—Texturizer

Grain

Ten Grain Types and two controls for Intensity and Contrast are offered here. In the Filter Gallery (see page 6), you can experiment by combining two or more grain patterns, and also vary their respective intensities. The initial grain types are similar to the results obtained from the Add Noise filter, but the latter types can produce some unique effects.

How it works

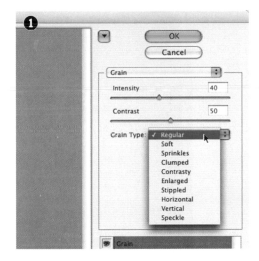

1, 2 The effects look familiar to Add Noise (see page 94), but with an immediate Blur function built in. The composite image above shows all ten grain types— the 11th strip is Film Grain from the Artistic suite (see page 18) for comparison.

Perhaps the most interesting Grain Types are the ones that don't actually produce traditional grain— such as Horizontal and Vertical, used here.

1, 2, 3 Duplicate the image, and apply the Horizontal Grain filter at Intensity 20, Contrast 55 to the upper layer. Immediately go to **Edit > Fade Grain** and reduce the effect to 75% in Overlay mode.

4 Hide the upper layer, activate the lower one, and re-apply the filter with the same settings but change the grain type to Vertical.

5 Immediately fade as before, activate the upper layer, and change its blending mode to Screen.

6 Try alternative blending modes of Overlay and Vivid Light for this result.

Craquelure

Compared with the filter effect, the patterns in real craquelure are more hard-edged, and each fragment shows signs of how it originally fitted to its neighbor. The filter uses a displacement map, so that most movement is present at contrast edges. To see how this works, try applying the filter to a plain background. The result will be a grid of squares, because there were no edges for the filter to work on. Real craquelure patterns tend to occur in different parts of an image depending on the paint that was used. One method of using this filter might be to select different color ranges in an image and then run the filter at different levels on the various colors selected.

How it works

1, 2 The built-in texture is revealed when run at Crack Spacing 30, Crack Depth 5, Crack brightness 8 on a plain 50% gray ground.

3, 4 Applied to the source image at the same settings, the filter shows few of the characteristics of real craquelure. Curiously, if you step back and re-apply the filter, the cracks will be in different places. (Incidentally, this filter is not affected by changes in the color palette.)

5, 6 Reduce the Crack Spacing to its minimum (2) for a cameo-like result. Zero the other two sliders for a brighter version.

7, 8 At stronger settings, you'll begin to see that the filter begins to follow the contours of the image. The rectilinear pattern is disturbed at strong contrast edges such as those around the lighthouse.

9 At the same settings, the target image shows similar displacement around the high-contrast central disk.

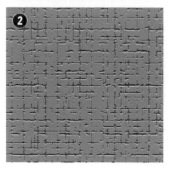

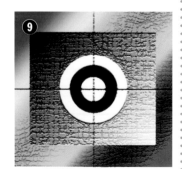

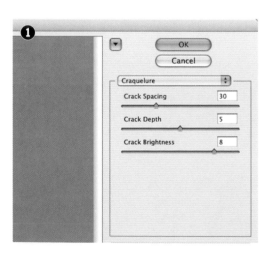

Real-world craquelure results from the differential expansion and contraction between paint and/or varnish layers and the canvas. It was so common in paintings in 18th-century England that it become known as "craquelure anglaise." This 19th-century example shows the effect on a folding screen decorated with printed scraps.

1 To reuse this natural pattern, choose the Lasso tool, with feather set at 8 pixels—the original here is about 2300 pixels wide. Use the Lasso tool to capture the most even and characteristic areas of craquelure, then Copy the captured selection.

2, 3 Make a new document about 1000 pixels square, and paste the copied fragment into it. Return to the original image, and select a different area. Copy and paste this as before. The new document will gain a layer each time you paste. Move the pasted objects around so that you can check your progress. As an alternative to copying, activating the new document, and then pasting, try just dragging the selection across to the new document window while holding down the Ctrl/ Cmd+Alt/Option keys.

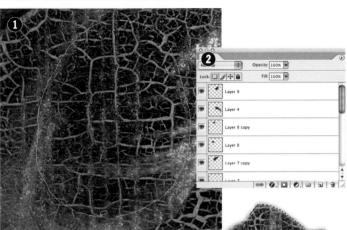

4, 5 Duplicate useful-looking layers (Ctrl/Cmd J) and use the Transform function to flip them horizontally or vertically (**Edit > Transform > Flip**). When this is done, flatten the image. Continue by using the Clone tool to cover over any gaps or obtrusive features, and extend the area covered.

6 When you have filled a reasonably even and square area, use the Crop tool to trim it. Make sure you have the Info palette visible (usually key F8) with the mouse coordinates set to pixels. Hold down Shift while you click and drag the crop tool and check in the Info palette that the cropped area is an even number of pixels square. Note the pixel dimensions and hit OK.

7 Select the Offset filter (**Filter > Other > Offset**), and enter half the pixel dimensions. This image is 660 pixels square, so 330 is the correct number.

8, 9 The effect can more easily be seen in closeup—there are newly formed edges halfway across and down the image where the pixels have been offset.

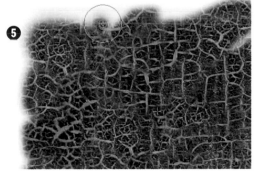

10 The task now is to eradicate these new edges, as the goal is to create a virtually seamless pattern. Use the Clone Stamp tool and the Healing Brush set to Soft Edges. Be careful not to alter areas close to the image edges, since they will already match perfectly when the pattern is used. In this particular case, look for "cracks" to clone that will neatly extend other cracks. In this 300% enlargement, the cross to the right is the source for the Stamp Clone tool, which is being used to produce a horizontal crack across the vertical edge.

11 When done, go to **Edit > Define Pattern**, give it a suitable name, and click OK.

12 To test the new pattern, make a new large document—say 3000 pixels square—go to **Edit > Fill**, and choose Custom Pattern from the fly-out palette. The fill will inevitably have some repeating characteristics, like the recurring lighter patches in this one. If they are troublesome, you can return to the original document and retouch some more (keeping away from the edges) and define the pattern again. Be aware, however, that overuse of the Clone Stamp and Healing Brush tool will eventually result in an undifferentiated mush of color.

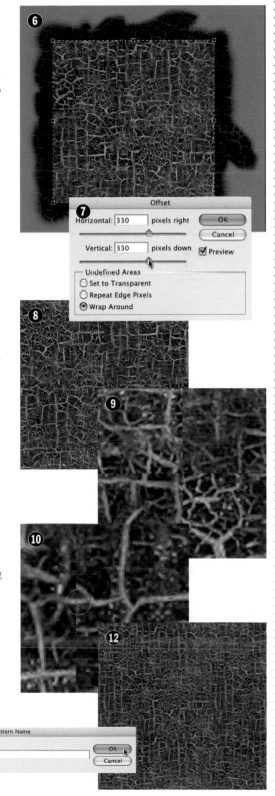

163

Mosaic Tiles

Mosaic Tiles superficially resembles the Craquelure filter, except that there is no displacement here. At large tile sizes, the individual elements approach squareness, while at medium and low settings they begin to resemble Craquelure's effect. The tile edges are a little too uneven and the pattern a little too regular for real mosaics, and of course the tesserae aren't single colors, but the effect does give an impression of painted tiles. See the following example for a better method of creating mosaics.

How it works

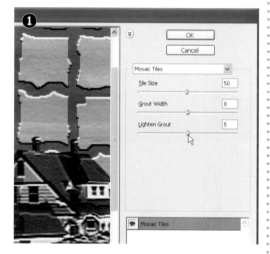

1 Tile Size is expressed in pixels, but the units for the other two sliders are rather more arbitrary.

2 The most useful setting turns out to be minimum Tile Size and Grout Width allied with the lightest possible grout color. The effect is somewhat like tempera paint on a rough gesso ground.

An alternative method of creating mosaic tiles

For a superior mosaic tile effect, try using the Patchwork filter.

1, 2, 3 Run the filter at maximum Size and minimum Relief. The closeup shows the immediate effect.

4 To create white grout, make a new top layer, and fill it with white (**Edit > Fill**). Re-apply the filter at the same settings (Ctrl/Cmd+F). The result should be a black grid on white ground.

5, 6 To increase the contrast, open the Levels dialog box (**Image > Adjustments > Levels**) and compress the sliders toward the top of the scale. Don't go right to the limit or the result will be overly hard-edged. Hit OK, then invert the result (Ctrl/Cmd+I).

7 Change this layer's blending mode to Screen.

8, 9 To add some relief to the tiles, duplicate the top layer, invert it and apply Emboss with minimum Relief. Change this new layer's blending mode to Overlay for a moderate result, or Vivid Light for something more strident.

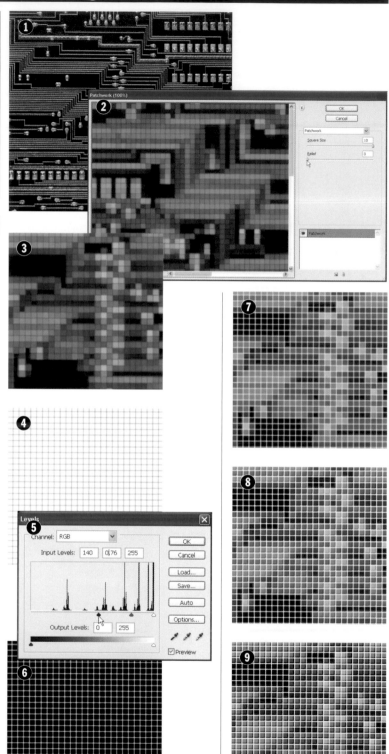

Stained Glass

tained Glass is similar to Crystallize in the Pixelate suite (see page 106) with the addition of a colored line around each cell (set according to the current foreground color). The effect is only faintly related to real stained glass. The Light Intensity slider attempts to aid the simulation by brightening the center of the image to emulate a light source shining through the glass. The loose mesh that is produced, though, is perhaps better used as a decorative background rather than a real representation of stained glass.

How it works

1 The source image here is around 450 pixels wide, so small values of Cell Size and Border Thickness are necessary. We've used Cell Size 6, Border Thickness 2, Light Intensity 6.

2 At the same settings, the pattern is revealed when used on a 50% gray area.

3 Flip the default palette to get "white lead." Remember to turn Light Intensity to minimum, or the central image will be blown out.

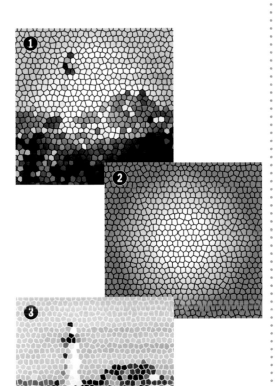

Traditional stained glass uses lead "cames," which outline the picture elements. Further decoration is often painted directly onto the glass. This technique aims to simulate the structure, but not the painting.

1, 2 Duplicate the image and blur the top layer slightly with a Radius of 10 pixels.

3 Run the Photocopy filter (in the Sketch suite) at maximum strength on the blurred layer. Turn off the background layer and, with the Eraser tool, erase the surplus small black marks that appear alongside the desired fat lines.

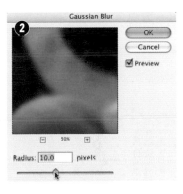

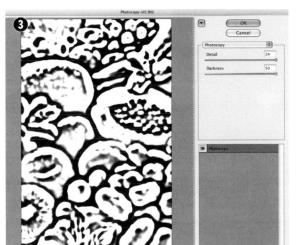

4, 5 Change the upper layer's blending mode to Multiply, add a new blank layer, and work on it with a soft black brush to improve the lead-work.

6, 7 Working on the same layer, Select All, and go to **Select > Modify > Border** and set Width to 50 pixels. Fill the resulting selection with black. You may need to repeat this operation several times to get a dense black frame. Deselect. Finally, blur the original image layer.

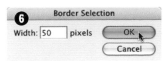

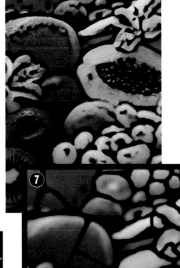

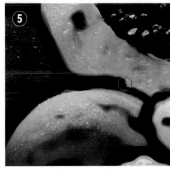

165

Patchwork

Results obtained with the Patchwork filter look almost nothing like real patchwork. There's a faint resemblance to the clipped pile of tufted rugs, but its ancestry lies more with its cousin, the Extrude filter. This relationship is evident in the way that light colors are raised and dark colors recessed in the image. See the following workthrough for an example of formal patchwork. Try the Pattern Maker (see page 184) to make a rag-rug simulation from any image of your choice.

How it works

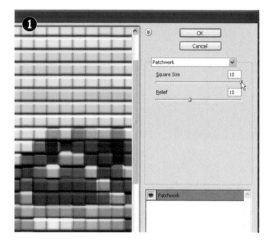

1 The maximum Square Size is 10, which is equal to around 15 pixels.

2 The Relief function brings lighter areas forward and depresses darker ones, though there is also an element of randomization.

3 With Relief set to zero, you have the beginnings of a good Mosaic Tile simulation.

4 Application to the target image shows that the perspective plot is upward and leftward, unlike the radial pattern of Extrude.

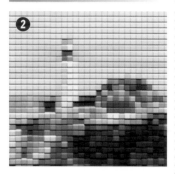

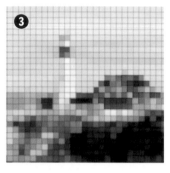

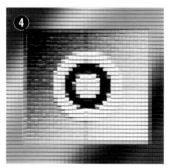

An alternative method of creating a patchwork effect

There are a range of templates available for the ardent patchworker, though many would rather work freehand. In this example, the image is angled to vary the effect of the applied texture, though there's no attempt to imitate the distinct pieces of different fabric in real patchwork.

1, 2 Duplicate the image twice. Apply the Texturizer filter to the top layer using Scaling 100, Relief 12, and set Texture to Canvas.

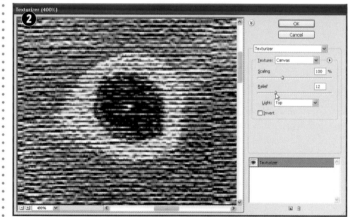

3, 4 Hide the top layer, activate the middle layer, and rotate the canvas 45° (**Image > Rotate Canvas > Arbitrary**). Apply the Texturizer filter again, and hide this layer.

5 Rotate the canvas another 45° (crop it to the original format now to save wasting processor time), and re-apply the Texturizer to the bottom layer. Finally, rotate the canvas back 90° counter-clockwise to the start point.

6 Click on the Create a New Layer icon at the foot of the Layers palette, reset the foreground and background colors (Key D), and fill the new blank top layer with white (Ctrl/Cmd+Backspace).

7 Run the Stained Glass filter. The preview window can be erratic at large cell sizes, so trial and error may be necessary to get the right number of cells. We have used Cell Size 45, Border Thickness 4, and Light Intensity 0 here.

8 Use Color Range in the Select menu to pick up the mesh of black lines. Change the top layer's blending mode to Multiply at this point, to make the subsequent steps easier.

9 With the selection active, hide the mesh layer and activate each image layer in turn, hitting Delete each time to make a narrow channel between the "patches," then deselect when they're all done.

10, 11 Activate the mesh layer and choose the Magic Wand tool (check Contiguous in the Tool Options bar). Make sure that Sample All Layers is unchecked. Select each of the patches in the mesh layer (hold down Shift to add patches to the selection). The idea is to delete around two-thirds of the patches in the uppermost of the three image layers. When you've selected enough patches, activate the uppermost image layer and hit delete. Check your progress by hiding all but the layer being worked on.

12, 13 Return to the mesh layer. Leave the uppermost image layer visible, and use the Magic Wand only in the white patches (those already deleted from the uppermost image layer). Select about half of them. Activate the middle image layer and hit Delete. Obviously, there's no need to treat the base layer. The closeup shows the result.

14, 15 Hide the mesh layer and merge the others (click on the fly-out button at the top-right of the Layers palette and choose Merge Visible). Click on the symbol at the foot of the Layers palette, and choose Bevel and Emboss. Change the Style and Technique to Pillow Emboss and Chisel Hard respectively. Changes can be made in the other values as well—especially to the Soften setting. Hit OK for the result.

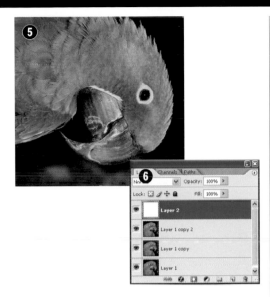

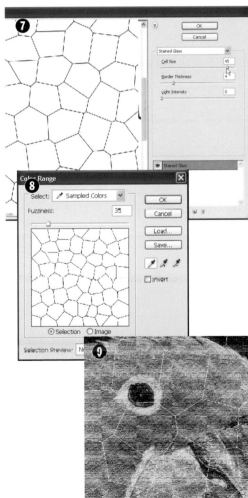

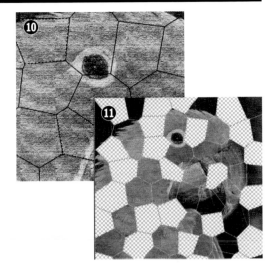

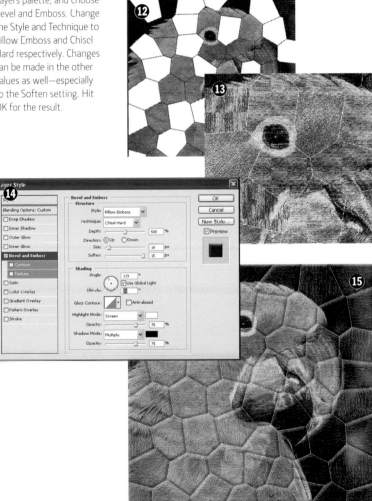

167

Texturizer

The familiar collection of Brick, Burlap, Canvas, and Sandstone also appear in the Conté Crayon, Glass, Rough Pastels, and Underpainting filters, and the mechanism is very similar. The difference is that the Texturizer filter solely adds the texture to the image rather than altering the image in any other way. You can create your own textures for use with this filter, and load them with the fly-out next to the Texture menu.

How it works

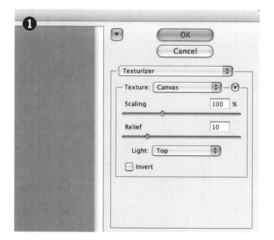

1, 2 With Scaling at 100%, the Canvas texture gives a convincing illusion.

3 For comparison, this composite has the four related filters at similar settings. From left to right: Conté Crayon, Glass, Rough Pastels, and Underpainting.

4, 5 For more grit, increase both Scaling and Relief. Here the Sandstone texture has been used, although the first result needed to be faded with Overlay.

6 Finally, here's the Burlap texture at maximum Relief and Scaling. The texture has almost totally replaced the underlying image.

Using the Texturizer filter

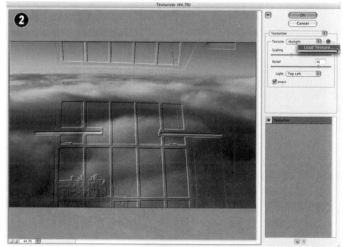

The Texturizer filter allows any Photoshop file to be used as a texture map. This includes the many built-in Photoshop files and any .psd documents you care to summon up.

1, 2, 3 Go straight to Load Texture, and navigate to the .psd file you want to use as a texture. In this case, the selected file is the source already used in the Spatter demonstration on page 69. Run Texturizer at Scaling 100%, Relief 40, Light Top Left, and tick the Invert box. Both images are of similar pixel dimensions.

4 The filter uses the contents of the first channel (Red in an RGB file, etc.) as a displacement map.

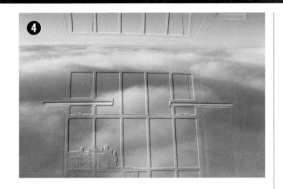

5 Repeating the operation with 50% Scaling gives the expected smaller result.

6 Here, the texture source image has been reduced to 20% of its original size, and used again at 50% scaling.

7, 8, 9 The imported file can even be used on itself, as long as scaling is kept to 100%. Although the Preview window gives a confused indication, the imported file fits perfectly.

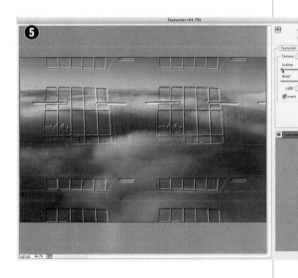

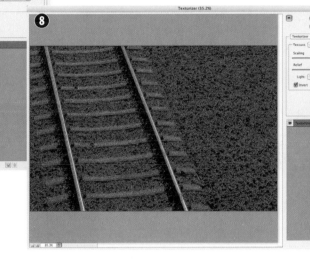

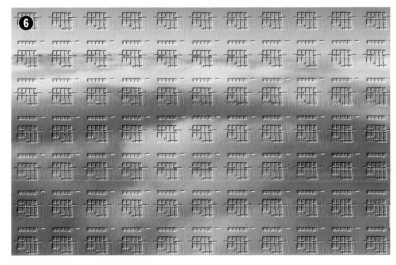

Other filters

Other filters

nder this dismissive heading lurk some useful items. Custom lets you design your own filter if you're unhappy with all of the built-in offerings (and the thousands of third-party filters and plug-ins). High Pass is a good way of isolating edges. Maximum and Minimum help out with modifying masks, and the last of the bunch, Offset, is a vital tool in producing seamless backgrounds and textures.

Video

he two filters in the Video suite have been superseded by more specialized functions within dedicated video-processing programs. They are only useful in enhancing grabs made from TV or telecine originals, or, more rarely, when exporting images made in Photoshop for re-purposing as TV or film.

De-Interlace

The TV image is typically produced by a horizontal scanning beam that enlivens half of the phosphors across the screen, then moves fractionally vertically to enliven the remainder. If a fast-moving subject is in view, its image will be displaced due to the time-lag between successive scans. De-Interlace aims to cure the problem by deleting the pixels of the first or second scan, and averaging, or simply duplicating, the remainder.

NTSC Colors

The NTSC Colors filter is a response to the limited gamut of the NTSC TV broadcast standard—easily recognized from the sometimes-odd rendition of intense reds, for example. The filter simply modifies the color image to fit the NTSC standard if you're exporting still Photoshop images to NTSC television.

170

page 171—High Pass

page 172—Custom

page 174—Maximum

page 174—Minimum

page 176—Offset

page 178—Extract

page 181—Liquify

page 184—Pattern Maker

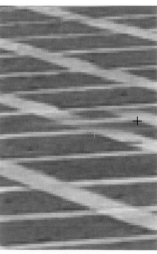
page 186—Vanishing Point

High Pass

You can use High Pass for preparing continuous-tone images for treatment as simulated line drawings. At low pixel values, it suppresses the image completely unless there are distinct color transitions which take place within the specified radius. The slider runs to 250 pixels, but is weighted toward the lower end of the scale. The upper end of the scale can still be useful, however, in producing sepia effects. Fine control can still be maintained at the upper end of the scale by using the cursor keys rather than the mouse to control the slider.

How it works

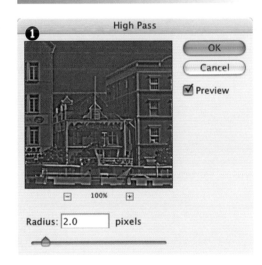

1, 2, 3, 4 The single slider runs from 0.1 (the active threshold for selecting edge pixels only) to 250 (just short of no effect at all). The examples here show the effect at pixel radius 2, 4, and 10 respectively.

5 The target image shows distinct edge effects at 2-pixels radius.

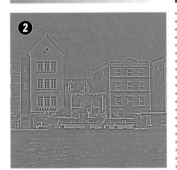

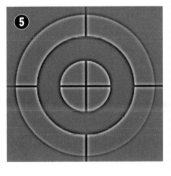

Using the High Pass filter

To give the various Photoshop high-contrast filters a head start, first pre-treat the image with the High Pass filter.

1, 2, 3 Small pixel radius values are enough to suppress unwanted detail.

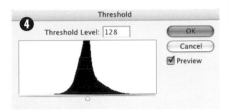

4, 5 Go to **Image > Adjustments > Threshold**. The default value of 128 works for this image.

6 As an alternative, run the Poster Edges filter and then fade using the Linear Light blending mode.

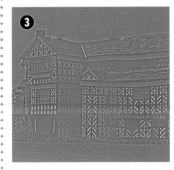

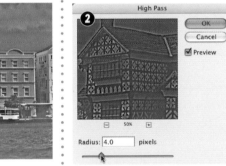

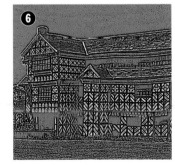

171

Custom

The basis of the Custom filter is the convolution kernel. It's represented in the dialog panel by a 5×5 matrix, which already has a few numbers entered into it. In use, one pixel in the image will have its brightness multiplied by the value in the central cell, then its immediate neighbors will be brightened (or darkened if it's a negative value) following the numbers entered in the relevant surrounding cells. In the default example, the central pixel is brightened by a factor of 5, and its four neighbors darkened by -1. Photoshop calculates a numerical value that is the total of the change to all five pixels. The value here is 1 (5 minus 4). It then divides the result by the figure in the Scale box. There's no effect in this case since that value is 1 by default. Finally it adds the value in the Offset box. Once again there's no effect since the default box has no value entered. The cumulative figure is the brightness value to be ascribed to the central pixel. This process is applied to every pixel selected.

How it works

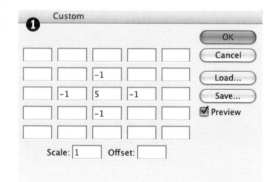

1, 2, 3, 4, 5 In this example, the default settings appear to sharpen the image. The effect is clearly seen by comparing the 400% close-ups before and after.

6 A closeup of the center of the target image shows the typical sharpening effect at work. The left side is unfiltered, the right filtered at the default settings.

7, 8 These 3-pixel square grids show the process at the pixel scale. The first is the unfiltered image, and the second has the default settings applied. The figures denote pixel brightness values.

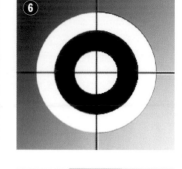

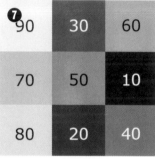

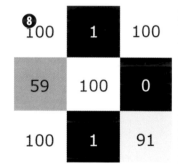

If you want to come to grips with the Custom filter matrix, you'll need an organized approach. Begin by saving some useful-looking settings, as they can be accessed again using the Load function. If everything gets out of control, you can always put the filter back to its default settings (shown in figure 1 on the previous page). Holding down the Alt/Option key and clicking Cancel in this instance will only return you to your previous settings.

1, 2 Compare the unfiltered image with the slightly sharper version produced by the default settings.

172

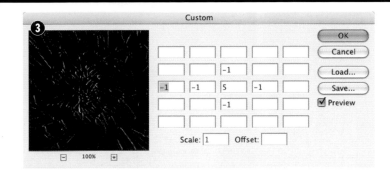

③

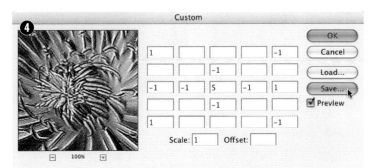

④

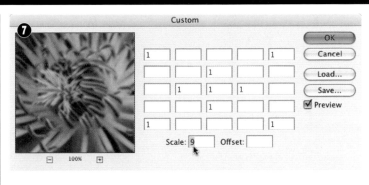

⑦

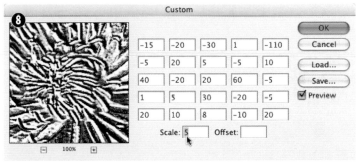

⑧

3, 4, 5, 6 Start slowly by making slight changes to the default settings. Just a minor addition to one cell completely changes the image—and not for the better in this case. The cure here is to balance out the effect across the matrix. Here three values of plus 1 have been symmetrically added with three minus values. It's crucial in this example that the product of all 11 numbers is still 1, thus preserving the existing image brightness. This setting can then be named and saved for re-use.

⑤

⑥

9

173

7 For the opposite effect— blur—return to the default settings and insert positive values symmetrically around the center cell. You'll see the preview image becoming extremely light. Instead of adding more values to restore the balance as before, just calculate the total product of all cells and insert the figure in the Scale box. If this won't bring the image within range, insert a value in the Offset box, and keep adding to it until you can see the image again, then adjust the Scale figure.

8, 9 This math exercise is all very interesting, but so far has achieved nothing that the native Blur and Sharpen filters cannot do ten times faster. How about an effect that doesn't already exist?

Half an hour spent adjusting values and checking the Preview window resulted in this effect. The product of these 25 numbers is 5, so we've used that as the Scale value. In the final version, we faded the new filter to 50% and then changed its blending mode to Linear Burn.

Maximum and Minimum

The Maximum filter spreads lighter areas at the expense of darker. Applied directly to a photographic subject, the filter has a drastic result at anything other than extremely low levels, although it can produce a pleasant shimmery, out-of-focus effect. This filter, as with the Minimum filter, is best applied to masks where it can be used to control the balance of light and dark area of the mask.

Operating in the direction opposite to Maximum, the Minimum filter spreads dark areas at the expense of lighter ones.

How it works

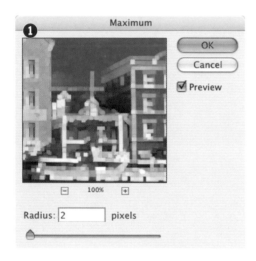

1, 2, 3, 4 There is an unexpectedly painterly look to results at low settings. These examples are at a pixel radius of 2, 4, and 10 respectively.

5 Even at 2-pixels radius, the target image has lost all of its line structure

6 The Minimum result is as expected, given the effect of its companion, Maximum, but no fortuitous painterly simulation here.

7, 8 Increasingly large blocks of black appear at 4 and 10-pixels radius respectively.

9 The 3-pixel wide lines of the target image are fattened to 7 pixels at Radius 2.

174

Maximum

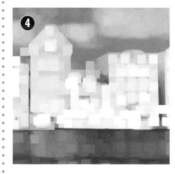

Minimum

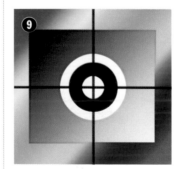

Maximum Demo

Maximum has a role in masking. The companion Minimum filter can be used if you prefer to produce a foreground, rather than a background, mask. The Maximum filter "chokes" white areas—expanding the parts that encroach on or spread into black areas. Minimum works in reverse, spreading out black and reducing white. The crucial point is that this is done by subtly shuffling pixels at the division between white and black, not by unilaterally increasing one area at the expense of the other.

1,2 In this RGB image, working in a close-up of the green channel (the one that usually displays most contrast) is the most direct route to separating the face from the background. Working with the Magic Wand tool, with Contiguous checked, a selection is gradually built up by clicking in the background with Shift held down. If you accidentally select part of the face, hit Ctrl/Cmd+Z to step back, then reduce the Magic Wand's tolerance, and continue clicking in the background. Large areas that are distant from the actual profile can be selected more easily with the Marquee or Lasso tools—still holding down Shift. Subtractions with all three tools are made by holding down the Alt/Option key.

3 With a reasonably complete selection, click on the Quick Mask icon in the Tools palette. The selected area will appear white in a new alpha channel at the foot of the Layers palette. Click on the eyeball icon to make the mask visible in the default red, then deselect.

4,5 Choose black as the foreground color, click in the alpha channel to activate it, and use a brush to repair any faulty areas. The brush, though black, will appear to paint in red. This repair work is often better done with just one color channel visible rather than the full RGB set.

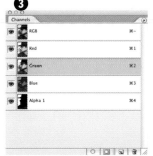

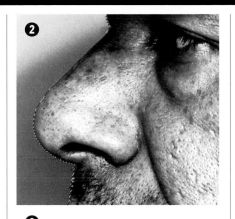

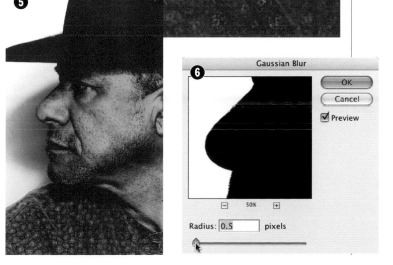

6 Hide all except the alpha, channel and open the Gaussian Blur filter. Since the Maximum filter only works in whole pixels, this is a good opportunity to first finesse the mask using a filter which offers one-tenth of a pixel increments.

7 Open the Maximum dialog box and apply the filter at minimum strength.

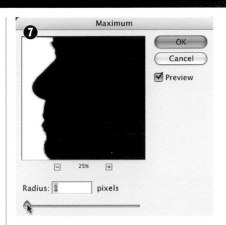

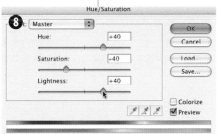

8, 9 Ctrl/Cmd+click on the alpha channel to obtain the selection, then hide the channel and move to the Layers palette. The background color can now easily be changed individually using, for example, the Hue/Saturation function.

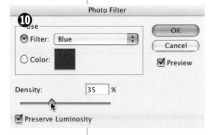

10, 11 Invert the selection (Ctrl/Cmd+Shift+I) to work on the figure. Photo Filter in the **Image > Adjustments** menu was used here to remove the yellow skin cast. While you're there, try out the other colored photo filters to familiarize yourself with their effects.

Offset

This filter can be used to move the image around on the canvas. The empty space produced by this movement can be filled through a number of means, similar to the options given with the Shear, Wave, and Distort filters. The maximum shift values allowed in the Offset dialog box are twice the relevant edge lengths. In addition to using the sliders to control the amount of offset, it's also possible to click on the image itself and drag that around on the canvas. The filter is useful for adding corner effects to an image—the image can be offset with Wrap Around so that the corners all meet in the center of the canvas; the desired effect can then be applied to all of the corners simultaneously (as they are now gathered together in the center), and the image can then be offset again to return it to normal.

How it works

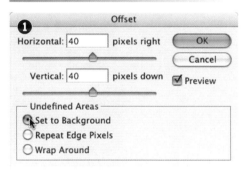

1, 2, 3, 4 There are three options for filling the space vacated by the offset image: Set to Background, Repeat Edge Pixels, and Wrap Around. They have very different results, so experiment to see which works best for your image.

Using the Offset filter

See page 163 for an example of using the Offset filter to create seamless patterns and texture maps. Here, we'll use the filter to create vibrant backgrounds.

1, 2, 3 The original has been cropped to 256 pixels square. Superficially, it appears to have a one-color background, but applying the Offset filter at 128 pixels in both axes shows that there is a variation.

4 We need to remove this background and replace it with a single color. Undo the filtration, and click the Eyedropper tool in the darker part of the background.

5 Go to Select > Color Range, select a low Fuzziness level, and click on the Add to Sample icon—the central eyedropper. Click this tool in the brighter part of the background. Hit OK.

6 With the selection active, go to Filter > Blur > Average. The slightly different light gray areas will be replaced with one single color.

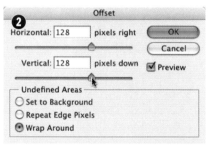

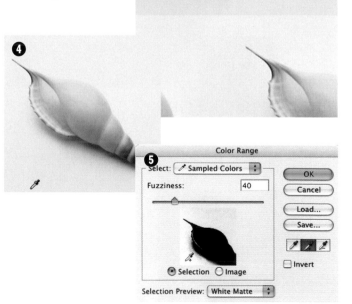

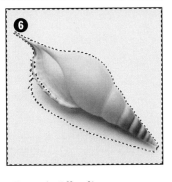

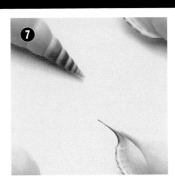

7 Re-run the Offset filter at the original settings. The boundary line is now absent.

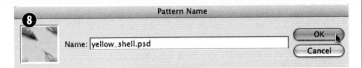

8 Go to **Edit > Define Pattern**. Give the pattern a new name, and then Click OK to save it.

9, 10 This pattern is now available from the Contents section of the **Edit > Fill** menu.

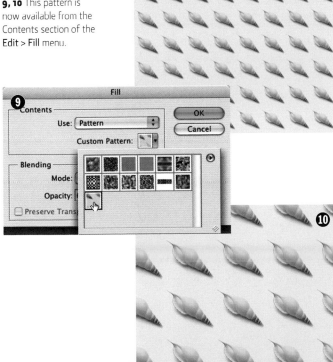

11 To get a denser pattern, capture the lower half of the image with the Rectangular Marquee tool, then hold down Ctrl/Cmd (and Shift to constrain the direction) and drag it up to approach the top half. Let go when it's in the right place, and deselect. Crop the document to this new image area.

12 To achieve even more density, select a portion of the right-hand side of the image (making sure that the selection edges only run through the averaged background areas). Hold down the Alt/Option key when selecting to subtract areas from the selection or Shift to add areas.

13, 14 Ctrl/Cmd+Shift and drag this selection to the left to take up the last of the unoccupied space. Let go and deselect when it's in the right place. Crop again to this reduced size. Be careful not to crop any pixels from the image edges.

15, 16 Follow the **Edit > Define Pattern** routine again to add this revised version to the Custom Pattern menu.

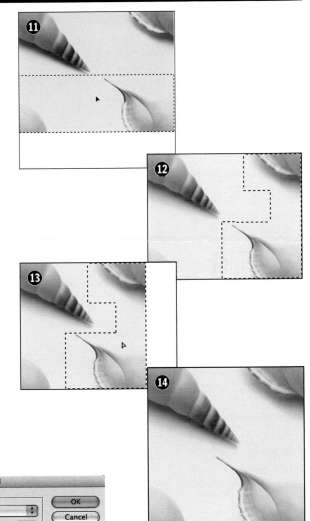

Extract

This complex filter—really more of an application in its own right—enables the separation of foreground and background in all but the most extreme cases. Try it on areas that are just too detailed to select by normal means.

How it works

1 The abbreviated toolbox contains tools as follows: Highlighter to define the edge to be extracted; Fill to flood the completed highlighted area; Eraser to delete mistaken highlighter lines; Eyedropper to select a foreground color (only available when Force Foreground—of which more later—has been selected); Cleanup tool to remove remaining fragments in the background area (hold down the Alt/Option key and use it to repair holes in the foreground object); Edge Touchup to sharpen the edges of the extracted object; Zoom in/out and the Hand to move around within the magnified image.

On the right side are found the Tool Options, which can be used to set the following: the radius of the Highlighter tool, its stroke color, the color of the eventual fill of the highlighted area, and the option to turn on the Smart Highlighting facility to look

for color edges. Just below the Tool options are the Extraction options: Textured Image to assist with differentiating strongly-textured foregrounds and/or backgrounds; Smooth to set the smoothness of the line tracing the edge of the extraction; Channel popup to allow a previously established alpha channel to be the basis of the highlight line; Force Foreground is for use when the subject is poorly defined relative to the background; and the color box, which accesses the color picker—an alternative to using the Eyedropper tool in the toolbox.

The Preview area includes a Show drop-down menu that toggles (only in Preview mode) between the extracted image and the original; Display, which offers a choice of matte styles; Show Highlight and Show Fill, which can be re-selected after Preview—they disappear by default when Preview is selected.

2 It's a good strategy to duplicate the source image before running Extract. In this way, you can easily compare the extracted with the original image, and add back detail from the original if you prefer not to use the History function. You may also find it useful to insert a strongly colored intervening layer against which you can minutely examine the extracted edge. This allows you to check on the white or light fragments which might otherwise escape attention. A similar facility is available within the Extract dialog box.

3 To make it easier to see darker fragments, you can set Grid Size to None in **Preferences > Transparency & Gamut**. Then, when you hide the underlying layers, you'll see the extracted edge against a white ground rather than against the usual checkerboard pattern.

4 Select the duplicated layer. You can choose to attack the whole image in one session, but it's usually less stressful to select a section at a time, especially where the target edges differ in character, and may need different treatment. Once you've made a selection, go to **Filter > Extract**.

5 You can toggle Smart Highlighting depending on the quality of the edge (just hold down the Ctrl/Cmd key to make the change). In this case, the upper section has a regular brush to highlight the width of the separate feathers of the crest. This was changed to smart highlighting to move along the well-defined edge of the beak. The smart line clings automatically to the edge, expanding wherever it becomes indistinct.

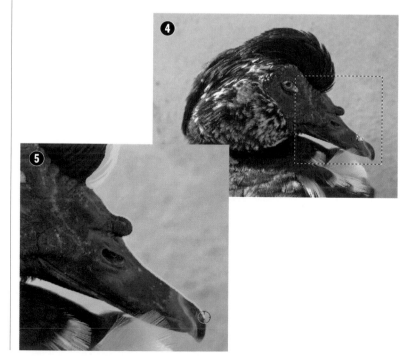

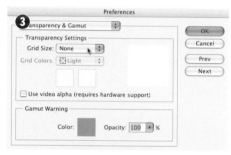

6 If you make a mistake, hit Ctrl/Cmd+Z to step back (only one step back is available). Otherwise, use the Eraser, then draw a better line. When the relevant edges have all been highlighted and you're sure the line is unbroken, choose the Fill tool, second from top, and click to fill the foreground area. The fill respects internal background areas such as that under the beak. If the highlight line is not complete, the whole frame will be flooded.

7 Click Preview to examine the result. The extracted image will appear against your selected transparency setting—the default light grid in this case. It's already clear that the extraction has worked well, except on the white feather area at the bottom edge.

8 To see the edge in more detail, click on the Display drop-down, and select Other. When the Color Picker appears, choose a color that isn't present in the original, and hit OK.

9 When you've selected the edges and checked the extraction in the preview, the choices are: accept the result by hitting OK, to go back, revise the highlighter line and re-fill; or to click on the Cleanup or Edge Touchup tools—they clean up traces in the background and reinforce the edge, respectively.

If you decide to revise the original Highlighter line, first check Show Highlight and Show Fill in the Preview box, then correct the line, re-fill, and preview it again. Alternatively, you can use the Cleanup tool in the background and the Edge Touchup tool on the

extracted edge. The closeups show the sharpening effect of the Edge Touchup tool. The white feather area looks beyond repair, and is a candidate for manual retouching using the regular eraser tool when the extract process is finished.

10, 11, 12 The closeup shows the next section to be treated—the lower right side of the image. Check the Textured Image option if the intended edge, or part of it, is textured like this. The Smooth setting, normally left at zero, will help to remove unwanted sharp artifacts at higher settings. A fat brush is used to include the whole edge area at once.

13 The result is a reasonably soft edge. The effect of the Extract filter can be further moderated by running the **Edit > Fade Extract** command with the blending mode changed to Luminosity.

14 Section-by-section, the edge is revealed.

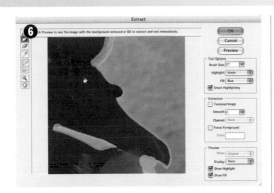

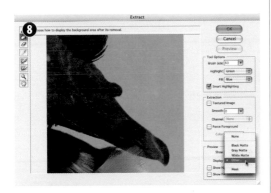

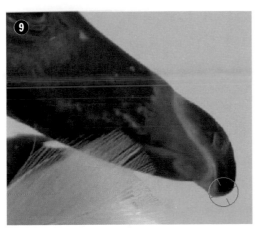

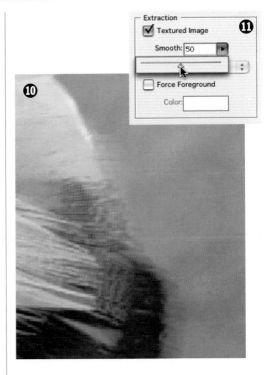

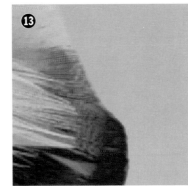

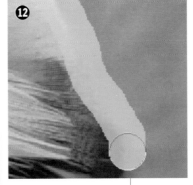

Extract FILTERS

15, 16 Inevitably, there is some retouching required after this semi-automatic process. Use the regular Eraser tool at a small size.

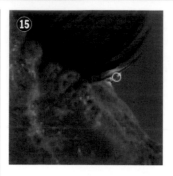

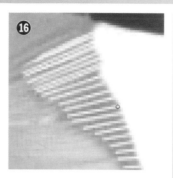

17 Find a suitable landscape image, then copy and paste it onto a new layer under the extracted duck layer.

18 To restore lost edge detail, hide all but the original and extracted layers, and use the Clone Stamp tool with Use All Layers selected, Alt/Option+click to select the source point and then begin painting with a very small brush tip at exactly the clicked point. Material from the original layer will begin to appear in the extracted image edge.
    You can also blur the extracted edge where it looks unnatural, and it can be helpful to use the Burn tool very sparingly to darken light edges. The final result is a convincing relocation.

19 In this second example, we'll use the Force Foreground function to extract only one color from the background image.

20 Open the image and select the Extract filter. Using the Eyedropper tool in the Extract window, click on the color that you want to extract, then check Force Foreground. Draw with the Edge Highlighter tool on the area you want to retain. The fill function is disabled and the filter just looks within the highlighted area for instances of the chosen color.

21 The preview shows that the chosen color and a few shades either side of it have been extracted. Although this method can be effective, it is often better done using **Select > Color Range**.

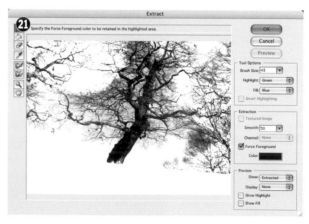

180

Liquify

A gentleman, according to old wisdom, was someone who knew how to play the piano-accordion, but didn't. Those equipped with this filter should show similar restraint by not using all its effects all at once—a little Liquify goes a long way.

How it works

1 The panel offers 12 functions in its toolbox, of which the first eight are directly concerned with distortion and reconstruction. The Freeze Mask tool paints a mask to protect areas from the filter's effects. Its companion, the Thaw Mask tool, has the opposite effect. The Move and Zoom tools work in the familiar way, and toggle between each other by means of the Alt/Option key. On the right side at the top are the Load Mesh and Save Mesh buttons, which enable favored distortions to be re-enacted on other images.

Tool Options control "brush" size, density, etc. Not all options are available to every tool—the Reconstruct Mode, for example, is only available when the Reconstruct tool is selected. Further down, the Reconstruct Options section controls the effects obtained by stepping back through the distortion sequence by hitting the Reconstruct button, rather than painting with the reconstruct tool. Five Mode types are available here from the popup, and these in turn can be varied in strength via the fly-out button at the right side. For each mode, a 0–100% slider will appear. Setting a value is not very rewarding, since it will revert to the default 30% after one

use. If you'd rather start over from the beginning, hit Restore All. Note that if you use the familiar "hold down Alt/Option while choosing Cancel" routine, the image will revert to its original state, but all tools will be reset as well.

Mask Options work with the Freeze Mask and Thaw Mask tools. The five pop-ups each reveal options to access either your original selection (only significant if you've made an irregularly shaped selection on which to apply the filter), or, if they are present in the document, the layer transparency, a layer mask, or an alpha channel. The pop-ups allow for these various sources to Replace, Add To, Subtract From, Intersect With, or Invert with respect to each other. You can then paint with the Freeze or Thaw tools to further modify the masked areas.

View Options has a useful Show Mesh checkbox with choices for Size and Color. In the next area, you can change the mask color and/or choose to hide it altogether. Finally, Show Backdrop lets you see the other layers, if any, in your document, to check them against the progress of the liquefied layer. You can even change the order, blending, and opacity of the layer stack (this doesn't affect the original) to get a better view.

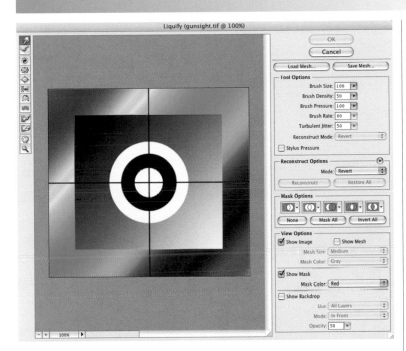

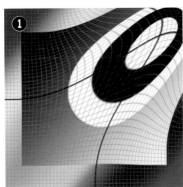

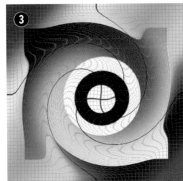

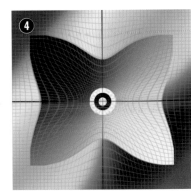

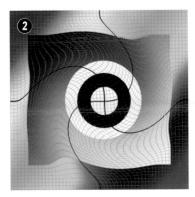

Forward Warp
Reconstruct
Twirl Clockwise
Pucker
Bloat
Push Left
Mirror
Turbulence
Freeze Mask
Thaw Mask
Move
Zoom

In the following examples of tools in use, the mesh image has been captured as well to make the distortion clearer. Unfortunately, there's no option to choose to retain the mesh image in normal use. The brush radius has been set to encompass almost the whole image, though all other values are at the default settings.

1 The Forward Warp tool clicked in the center of the target, then Shift+clicked at the top right corner.

2 The Twirl tool after approximately five seconds' application at the center of the target. Hold down the Alt/Option key to reverse the direction of rotation.

3 The Twirl tool after ten seconds' application.

4 The Pucker tool after five seconds' application at the center of the target. Hold down Alt/Option to change it to the Bloat tool.

181

5 The Pucker tool after ten seconds' application.

6 The Bloat tool after five seconds' application at the center of the target. Hold down Alt/Option to change it to the Pucker tool.

7 The Bloat tool after ten seconds' application.

8 The Push Left tool clicked in the center of the target, then Shift+clicked horizontally to the right side. Moving to the right pushes the image upward; moving left, vice-versa. Hold down Alt/Option to reverse these functions.

9 The Mirror tool clicked in the center of the target, then Shift+clicked horizontally to the right side.

10 The Turbulence tool after five seconds' application at the center of the target.

11 The Turbulence tool after ten seconds' application.

12 If you need to mask ("freeze" in Liquify's terms) a part of your image, accurate selection and masking is better done in the regular Photoshop workspace prior to filtering. Here, an alpha channel is used to mask all but the central strip of the image, and has been accessed using the Replace Selection pop-up in the mask options section. Show Mask is checked to reveal it.

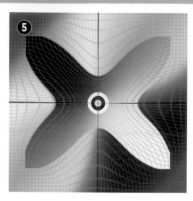

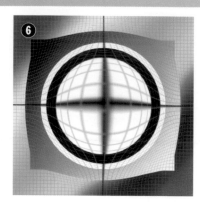

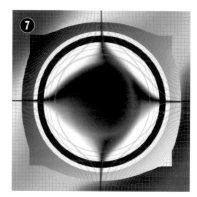

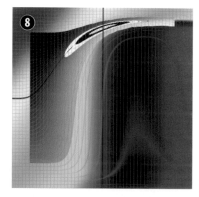

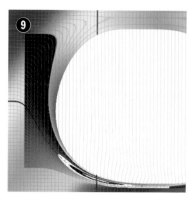

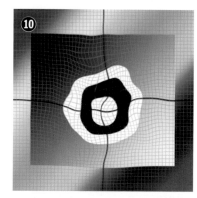

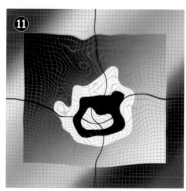

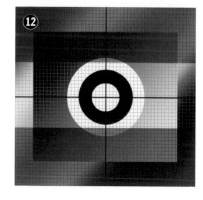

13 As a result, the effect of the Twirl filter is confined to the central strip.

14 With the addition of a second alpha channel, this time with a strip running vertically, the combined mask produces a cross-shaped "unfrozen" section.

15 With the Twirl tool used once more, only the corner sections escape treatment.

16 With the Thaw tool, you can modify the mask. Increase the Brush Density figure to get a harder edge, and trim away some of the mask. It's now clear why it's better to finesse the mask before filtering.

17 The Twirl tool now reaches into the recently shaved-off corners.

18 A fairground ride that naturally appears quite liquified is an ideal subject.

19 A Lasso selection to preserve the road surface and surroundings was made into a layer mask using Quick Mask (click on the mask icon at the foot of the Layers palette) and the Liquify filter applied. The mask was then selected within Liquify.

20 All of the available tools were employed in distorting the image. Here, the Twirl tool gets to work on the marquee sign.

21 Inevitably the distortions sometimes get a little out of control and affect areas that you don't want to distort.

22 The Reconstruct tool returns the image to its original state, or a halfway

stage, depending on how long you apply it.

23 When the "eyes" appeared by chance after an application of the Twirl tool, a halt was called, leaving this somewhat macabre result.

24 With the image view turned off, the distorted mesh can be showed by itself, revealing the full extent of our actions.

25, 26 You can save the mesh for re-use, though in this case there's little point, since it's very specific to this image. Just for the record, it has been re-applied here to a country cottage. However, a simpler mesh might be a better candidate for saving to use on alternate images.

27, 28 A note on Reconstruct modes: the reconstruct tool has eight different Reconstruct modes. In practice, you probably just need two—the ordinary Revert, which returns the image to normal as you paint across the distortions, and, for creating random effects, Amplitwist.

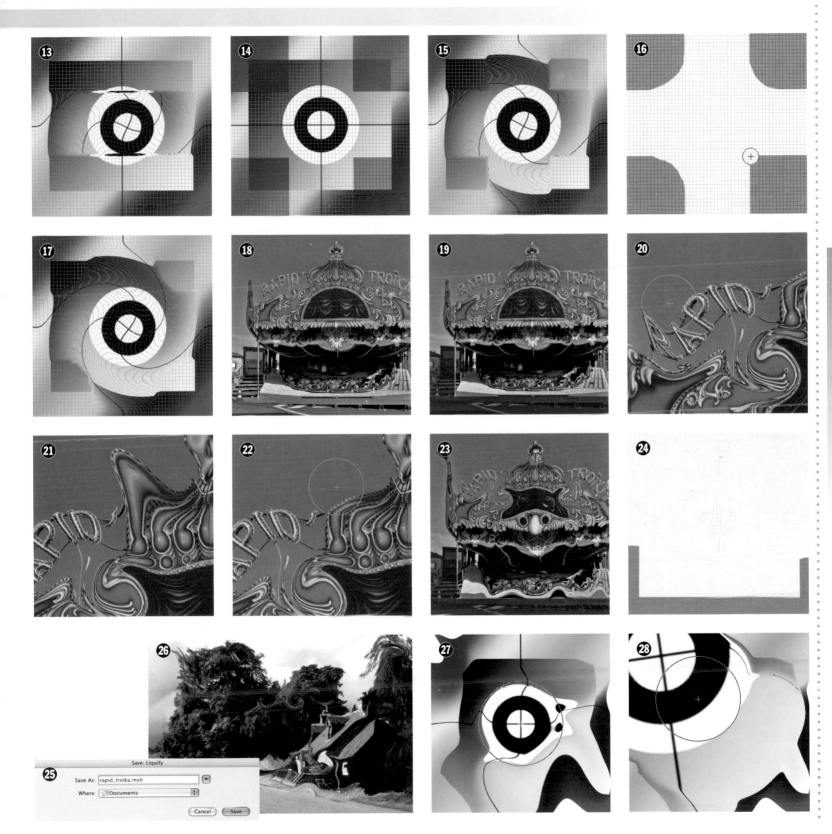

Pattern Maker

The Pattern Maker filter offers two distinct approaches. You can choose to simply let the filter randomly slice up and re-arrange your original, or to use all or part of it as the starting point for saved patterns. These patterns can then be applied to other images via the Edit > Fill command. The slicing-up route can give you good results, sometime useful for decorative backgrounds, and it's very quick to operate, unless you start seriously modifying the default settings. The "making a pattern" route needs a more studied approach, but there's similar pleasure to be had just mindlessly generating patterns, until a chance combination hits the spot.

Be aware that in either case you won't get a seamless result. See pages 176 and 162 for details on how to use the Offset filter to produce seamless patterns. Try using one of the built-in Photoshop images to get familiar with Pattern Maker.

How it works

1, 2 This example is Spiky Bush, which you'll find in the Textures folder inside Photoshop's Presets folder. If you haven't made a selection of all or part of the image before opening the filter, then you'll receive an alert message. You can then make a selection with the Marquee tool at top-left of the panel. Click Generate when you've selected the required area.

3 Looking more closely at the filter controls, you'll see Use Clipboard as Sample as an option under Tile Generation. To use this option, copy part or all of a different image to the clipboard, then open your target image, open the filter, and check the option. In this way, you'll cover the target with a pattern derived from the secondary image.

You can control the pattern tile size in the same area. Choose Use Image Size to make one large tile, or reduce the size using the Width and Height selectors. Inevitably, smaller tiles are generated more quickly. By default, tiles are produced on a rectilinear grid pattern. To offset tiles, click on the Offset button and insert values for Horizontal and Vertical offset. Increasing the value of the Smoothness control helps to reduce the appearance of sharp edges in the generated pattern; similarly, increasing Sample Detail gives a richer pattern, based on more information from the source image.

In the Preview area, Show allows you to switch the view between generated tiles and your original; you can also choose to make the tile boundaries visible. The Tile History area contains the 20-shot viewer of

unsaved patterns, equipped with player controls, a Save, and a Trash function.

The Update Pattern Preview checkbox is significant only when you are using the player to review the tiles you've already made. If it's checked, the main preview window will show the selected tile used as a pattern—if unchecked, the preview screen does not refresh.

4 You can hit Generate Again up to 19 times before getting this warning dialog.

5 If you keep going regardless, the newest pattern will replace the oldest, always keeping 20 tiles in the viewer. Click on the Trash icon to delete unwanted tiles or, as here, the Save icon to keep them.

6 When the Pattern Name dialog appears, you can choose a name or just hit OK, in which case the new tile will be named Pattern 1, the next one Pattern 2, and so on. If you're done creating tiles and don't want to apply the newest pattern to your original, hit Cancel. The saved tiles you made will be preserved and you'll be returned to an untouched original.

7, 8 Next time you visit the **Edit > Fill** dialog and choose Use Pattern, you'll see the new pattern as an addition to the default set. It shows the characteristic banding when applied to a large area.

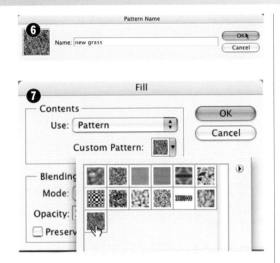

9 A more direct alternative is to select part of your original image and use it to produce a deliberately variegated pattern. A small section of this picture of Italian cyclists riding through Egypt makes a suitably colorful starting point.

185

10 20 attempts, with only the Offset value changed from the default value, gives a typically frantic result.

11 Alternatively, return to the original image, select all, and run the Pattern Generator again, but this time click the Use Image Size button. Increase Smoothness to maximum, insert a larger value for Sample Detail and introduce some Offset.

Vanishing Point

Introduced in Photoshop CS2, the Vanishing Point filter is a plugin that has its roots in the Clone Stamp tool, but is flexible enough to deal with the effect of perspective. Photographers who have traditionally waited hours for the departure of people, vehicles and various wildlife from photogenic plazas can now shoot immediately, secure in the knowledge that a few minutes' work in Photoshop is all that's needed to clear the streets.

How it works

186

1 To experiment with Vanishing Point, select an image that has a clear perspective plane. Uniform paving slabs are an enormous help. The initial intention here is humble—just to eliminate the street lamp shadows.

2 Duplicate the image and add a blank layer as well by clicking on the "Create a new layer" icon at the bottom of the Layers palette—make this the active (target) layer. The filtration will be carried out on the image layer (even though it's apparently inactive). Vanishing Point will deposit the filtered version in the blank layer as long as it is active. It's the only filter in Photoshop that will perform this useful trick.

3 Open the Vanishing Point filter. The toolbox contains nine items of which the first two—Edit Plane and Create Plane—are, for now, the most important. The remaining tools, apart from the familiar Hand and Zoom tools, only come into play once the reference plane has been created. The extensive list of view size options, accessed from the fly-out at the foot of the window, gives a clue to the importance of accurate positioning when using this filter. Alongside the fly-out is a small bar that will later register the progress of rendering—this is one of the more memory-intensive filters in the suite.

4 Accuracy in creating the initial plane is absolutely crucial to the success of this filter. Using the Create Plane tool, click on an obvious reference point, then drag to another one on the same axis, click again and look for a point on the opposite axis.

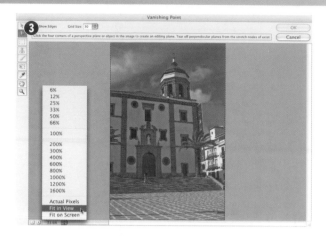

image contains no clearly defined planes. It's much better for general use to rely on accurately plotting the nodes by hand.

7 If you see a red or yellow grid, your plotting is outside acceptable norms. Yellow is more unacceptable than red, but both mean you should correct the plane to accord with the image.

Hold down the X key whenever you like during this process—it will zoom to a double-size view and back to the original size when released. As soon as you've clicked on three points, a fourth node will be generated automatically. Drag this node to the last corner of the plane and release the mouse button.

5 A "good" grid will appear in blue, confirming that it is valid in the filter's general perspective terms.

6 Note that the appearance of the blue grid does not mean that it necessarily fits your particular image. Use the topmost tool —Edit Plane—to drag a node to an obviously "wrong" point and you'll see the grid remaining resolutely blue. The color check is useful when the

8 The finished grid has a node mid-way (in perspective terms) along each edge. Use the Edit Plane tool to drag these nodes out toward, and beyond, the image edges. This is an opportunity to check the grid against a wider sample of the image. If it fits all round, fine; if not, use the Edit Plane tool on the corner nodes to correct it. Any corrections made at

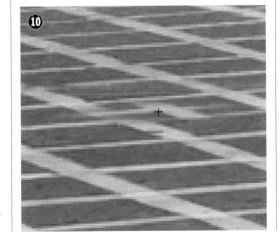

this point will be beneficial, especially if tear-off planes (see below) are to be used.

9 With the blue grid active, select the Stamp tool. The grid lines disappear, leaving just the plane edges. A Tool Options bar appears at the top of the window with options for the Stamp tool. Choose Aligned and, in this case, Off for the Heal option, since there is little color variation in the courtyard area, and the intention is for all of the tiles to look similar.

10 Alt/Option+click within the grid area to establish the cloning source point. The

edges of the plane change to green. In this case, choosing the junction between two tiles gives a good starting point. In this much enlarged view, the green cross represents the clicked source point, the black cross the center of a hovering, feathered selection. It's effectively a "loaded brush," ready to paint just like the conventional clone stamp tool, except that it will operate in perspective.

11 Position the selection where needed, carefully aligning it with a similar junction in the tiles. Zoom in if necessary using the Zoom tool, and click to establish the "brush." Paint over all of the areas to be treated. You can go back one step at a time by hitting Ctrl/Cmd+Z if things aren't working out. If you want to choose a different source point, there is a minor problem—the

existing loaded brush will obscure the intended new source point. The core is to set the opacity in the contextual menu to 0% while you reset the source point, and then restore it to 100% when you are done. Here, the source point (the green cross) in the background is supplying the image data used to obscure the street lamp shadow in the foreground.

12 Finally, the shadows are all painted out. It was necessary to reset the source point several times to allow for local irregularities in the tiling. Hit OK when done.

13 If you set an empty layer to receive the retouched areas (see step 2), you can check the results with the original layer hidden.

187

Vanishing Point

14, 15 You can deal with other plane areas in the image in the same way. Ideally this should be done using a tear-off plane (see the following example) but in this case it's simpler to set up a new one. Start by selecting the area to be modified. This will prevent unwanted alteration of surrounding areas. Open the Vanishing Point filter (you'll notice that the original plane helpfully re-appears) and set up a new, vertical plane.

16 Check and stretch this plane as before, and zoom in on the selected area. Select the Stamp tool, and Alt/Option-click on a suitable source point. Here, a junction in the brickwork is selected and the cloned area positioned over the target. Click and paint as before. Although it's tempting to choose a large brush and attempt to retouch extensive areas all at once, the cloned area will inevitably contain unwanted elements which will, in turn, need to be retouched.

17 It's possible to isolate progressively smaller areas within their own planes. This balustrade, for example, can be laboriously cloned from the small section which remained unobstructed by the palm tree. The choice between the three Heal modes will depend on the type of area being cloned. Ctrl/Cmd+Z enables you to step back quickly if you choose the wrong one.

18 Image elements that cannot be re-created by cloning within the Vanishing Point filter will need some conventional retouching.

Here, the Vanishing Point filter came to the rescue when a rectangular, vertically formatted brochure had to be covered, but only a square source image was available.

1, 2 Prepare the ground by selecting **Image > Canvas Size** and increasing the height of the canvas size by the required amount (here, it was 150%) to get more space at the top of the frame. Create a new blank active layer by clicking "Create a new layer" at the bottom of the Layers palette to receive the filtered result.

3 Open the Vanishing Point filter, and draw a plane on one face of the building.

4 Having made sure the nodes align, hold down the Ctrl/Cmd key and drag the midpoint node sideways to "tear off" a perpendicular plane. The nodes on this new plane will need to be aligned, using the Edit Plane tool, with the relevant points on the building.

5 Moving these nodes may in turn displace some of the existing nodes. Use the tool to correct them as well.

6 Select the Marquee tool (third from the top) and select the upper floors of the building. The relevant plane will now show a thicker edge to confirm the plane of selection.

7 If the selection is incorrect, you'll have to deselect it (Ctrl/Cmd+D, or click elsewhere) since there's no adjustment available. Once it's correct, hold down Alt/Option, click, and drag it upward.

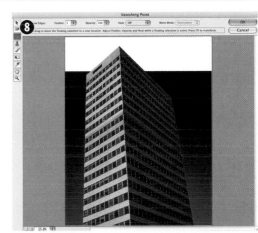

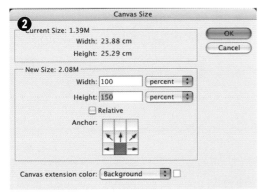

189

8 Repeat on the other face. Here, the selection marquee has been hidden (Ctrl/Cmd+H) to make the operation easier. Hit OK when you're done.

9, 10 The formerly blank layer show the results of the maneuver. You can add more sky in the background layer to fill up the canvas, using the regular Clone and Healing Brush tools, or just replace the entire sky with a new gradient.

Index

INDEX

Acknowledgments

Dedicated to Sarah, Sally, and Katy.

Photography by Roger Pring and photos.com. Additional images courtesy of Mary Tiegreen and Christopher Cormack.

192